W9-BFG-515

Country Christmas

*Somehow,
a place of country quiet,
with livestock crunching on its feed,
with sheds and barns and corncribs,
with crop and pasture land rolling away serenely,
their shape clearer in winter
under the defining snow,
seemed the best of all possible places
to celebrate this holiday
begun in a little village
in sheep-raising country
on the other side of the world.*

Paul Engle, *An Iowa Christmas*

Ideals Publishing Corporation
Nashville, Tennessee

Publisher, Patricia A. Pingry; Editor, Nancy J. Skarmeas; Art Director, Patrick T. McRae;
Copy Editors, Tim Hamling and Donna Sigalos Budjenska
Design and Nature Art by Susan Harrison

Acknowledgments

CHRISTMAS FERNS by Hal Borland. Reprinted by permission of Frances Collin, Literary Agent. Copyright ©
1957 by Hal Borland. Copyright © renewed 1985 by Barbara Dodge Borland; DECEMBER by Hal Borland.
Reprinted by permission of Frances Collin, Literary Agent. Copyright © 1957 by Hal Borland. Copyright ©
renewed 1985 by Barbara Dodge Borland; FESTIVE DECEMBER by Gladys Taber. Copyright © 1977 by The
Family Circle, Inc. Reprinted by permission of Brandt & Brandt Literary Agents, Inc.; KEEPING CHRISTMAS by
Henry Van Dyke. Reprinted with the permission of Charles Scribner's Sons, an imprint of Macmillan Publishing
Company from *THE SPIRIT OF CHRISTMAS* by Henry Van Dyke. Copyright © 1905 Charles Scribner's Sons.
Copyright © renewed 1933 Ellen Reid Van Dyke; A MISERABLE, MERRY CHRISTMAS from *THE AUTOBIOG-
RAPHY OF LINCOLN STEFFANS, VOLUME I*, by Lincoln Steffans, copyright © 1931 by Harcourt Brace
Jovanovich, Inc. and renewed 1958 by Peter Steffans, reprinted by permission of the publisher; SIMPLICITY by
Hal Borland. Reprinted by permission of Frances Collin, Literary Agent. Copyright © 1957 by Hal Borland.
Copyright © renewed 1985 by Barbara Dodge Borland; SKATING POND by Edna Jaques. © in Canada by
Thomas Allen & Son Limited; Our sincere thanks to the following authors whom we were unable to locate:
Lynda Bearden for CHRISTMAS IS A THOUSAND THINGS; Ada B. Childs for THE CAROLERS; Reverend John
W. Fehringer for CHRISTMAS EVE; Harriet Feltham for IT'S CHRISTMASTIME; Ruth B. Field for COUNTRY
CHURCH AT CHRISTMASTIME; Viola B. Gore for WHY THE ROBIN'S BREAST IS RED; Mildred L. Jarrell for
WOODLAND SOLITUDE; Elisabeth Johnson for MANGER SCENE; Elizabeth Landeweer for LO! THE LIGHT!;
Agnes B. Nickl for THE CHRISTMAS CANDLE LEGEND; Adam N. Reiter for GRANDMOTHER'S HOUSE; Grace
V. Watkins for THE HEART GOES HOME; Diana Smith Watts for CHRISTMAS IS; Helen Welshimer for NOT
FORGOTTEN.

Copyright © 1992 by Ideals Publishing Corporation, Nashville, Tennessee

All rights reserved. No part of this publication may be reproduced or transmitted in any form or by any means,
electronic or mechanical, including photocopy, recording, or any information storage or retrieval system, without permission in writing from the publisher.

Text copy set in Berkeley; Display type set in Belwe Medium
Printed and bound by Ringier America, Milwaukee, Wisconsin

ISBN 0-8249-4050-4

COVER ART
HOME FOR CHRISTMAS
LINDA NELSON STOCKS

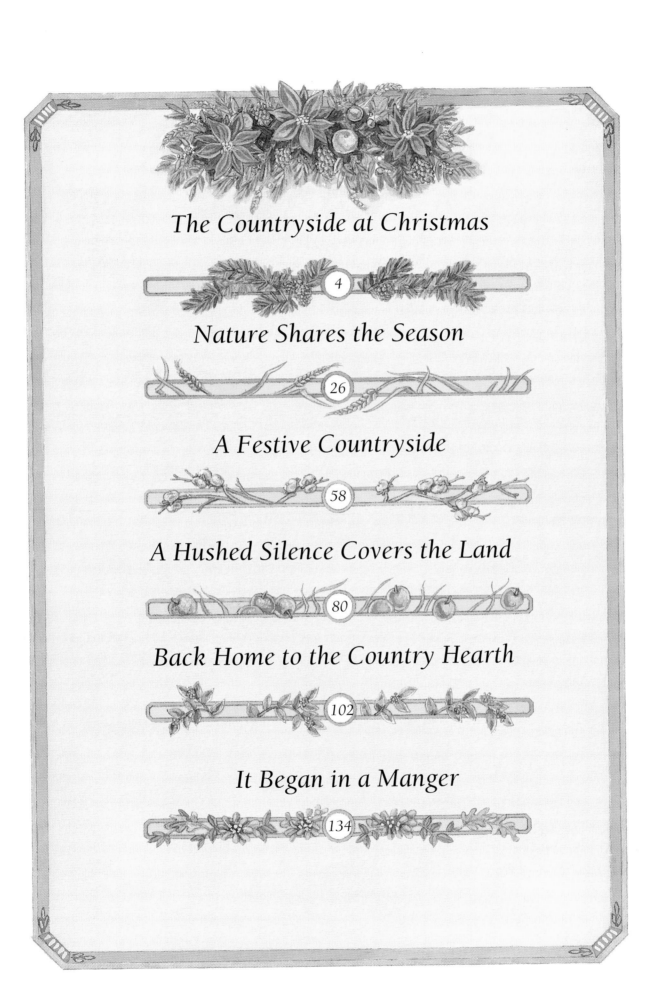

The Countryside at Christmas

4

Nature Shares the Season

26

A Festive Countryside

58

A Hushed Silence Covers the Land

80

Back Home to the Country Hearth

102

It Began in a Manger

134

THE COUNTRYSIDE AT CHRISTMAS

PINE TREE
TAVERN

Candles in the Window
LINDA NELSON STOCKS

5

It's Christmastime

Harriet Feltham

It's Christmastime, it's Christmastime,
The church bells say in every chime:
A time for work and care to cease:
Give praises to the Prince of Peace.

It's Christmastime, it's Christmastime,
A day for joy in every clime,
A day to celebrate a child's birth
And foster peace upon this earth.

The fir trees shine with glowing light,
To cheer a stranger through the night,
Reminding him of brotherhood,
Of faith, of love, and all that's good.

Carols ring through cold, crisp air;
Families gather everywhere;
And up above the stars do shine
Much brighter—'cause it's Christmastime!

THE BEAUTY OF WINTER AT PARADISE PARK,
MT. RAINIER NATIONAL PARK, WASHINGTON

An Iowa Christmas

Paul Engle

Every Christmas should begin with the sound of bells, and when I was a child mine always did. But they were sleighbells, not church bells, for we lived in a part of Cedar Rapids, Iowa, where there were no churches. My bells were on my father's team of horses as he drove up to our horse-headed hitching post with the bobsled that would take us to celebrate Christmas on the family farm ten miles out in the country. My father would bring the team down Fifth Avenue at a smart trot, flicking his whip over the horses' rumps and making the bells double their light, thin jangling over the snow. . . .

A bobsled was the wonderful and proper way to travel on Christmas morning. The space it offered was generous, just like the holiday itself. There was no crowding on narrow seats where children had to sit upright. Instead, the long, wide body of the sled allowed us such comfort and freedom as no car or plane can give.

In that abundant dimension, we could all burrow down under the clean-smelling straw, pull a shaggy robe over us, and travel warm and snug while still being outdoors with the wind in our faces.

On a level piece of road, Father would collect the reins firmly, cluck to the team, snap the whip over their ears, and settle them into a fast trot, bells jangling in celebration, runner clacking, and the children yelling with the speed and sway of it.

There are no streets like that any more: the snow sensibly left on the road for the sake of sleighs and easy travel. And along the streets we met other horses, so that we moved from one set of bells to another, from the tiny tinkle of individual bells on the shatts to the silvery, leaping sound of the long strands hung over the harness. There would be an occasional brass-mounted automobile laboring on its narrow tires, and as often as not pulled up the slippery hills by a horse, and we would pass it with a triumphant shout for an awkward nuisance which was obviously not here to stay. . . .

The country road ran through a landscape of little hills and shallow valleys and heavy groves of timber, including one of great towering black walnut trees which were all cut down later to be made into gunstocks for the first World War. The great moment was when we left the road and turned up the long lane to the farm. It ran through fields where watermelons were always planted in the summer because of the fine, sandy soil, and I could go out and break one open to see its Christmas colors of red and green inside. My grandfather had been given that farm as bounty land for service as a cavalryman in the Civil War.

BELGIUM DRAW HORSE AND SLEIGH,
EDSOM HILL MANOR, STOWE, VERMONT

My uncle, Mother's brother, and our cousins lived on the same place where Mother had been born. Somehow, a place of country quiet, with livestock crunching on its feed, with sheds and barns and corncribs, with crop and pasture land rolling away serenely, their shape clearer in winter under the defining snow, seemed the best of all possible places to celebrate this holiday begun in a little village in sheep-raising country on the other side of the world.

A NEW ENGLAND VILLAGE SETTLES IN FOR THE WINTER,
EAST TOPSHAM, VERMONT

Christmas Is
the Best Day of Winter

Rosalyn Hart Finch

Winter came boldly to town again this year, frosting the clammy streets and sifting bleary halos around the pole lights. Wrapped in cold, nose-stinging air, winter brushed its frosty hands all over the trees, favoring none more than others. Nude branches, as well as the plushy, needle-covered fir limbs, are exquisite in their ice-lustered spangles.

Here and there happy souls take secret little slides, adults choosing out-of-the-way spots, youngsters daring on the very face of the town itself. The crisp air enters the bloodstream as instant, invigorating current, urging one to walk out among the newly revealed secrets kept hidden all summer long; shaggy, high-rise bird apartments nested overhead, shiny red berries decorating withered brown forest limbs, the winding, seeking, formerly green-shrouded courses of creek and river now swelling ice-clad shoulders to their banks.

We are all charged with expectations, for we know that winter's specialty, heavy snowfall, is not far away. Does the snow fail to stir any of our imaginations? Or will we merely gaze in awe at its dazzling descent, remembering similar times of wonder? Won't that nameless feeling of pleasure we all experience at suddenly awakening to a fresh, soft, white world brighten some of the humdrum hours of living and put a new face on dispositions?

Certainly, during the holiday season, winter interweaves a jovial spirit into everything. It puts a bloom on the cheeks of small fry and oldsters alike. Folks look healthier with their ruddy complexions. Cheerful tones and happy words crowd the air, bidding to outdo one another.

Even indoors, winter exerts its delicious side effects. Domesticity takes on fresh charm with burning logs snapping in the fireplace, their glow reflected in the faces of our loved ones. Slippered feet prop contentedly on couches and footstools. Small sips of steaming hot cocoa or coffee seem to contain soothing spirits of tranquilizing secrets.

Yes, winter is here. Thank God for winter. Without her we might never have been introduced to the thoroughly delightful meaning of coziness.

Now in winter's clutches we are not struggling, for we look to her highest pinnacle, Christmas. Christmas is the best day of winter and of the whole year for most of us. On this day we will call to our minds and hearts the very tenderest of thoughts about friends far and near. On this day we will feel able to consider forgiveness for all our past hurts, big and little. We will ferret out large supplies of generosity which have lain dormant throughout the rest of the year, and spread them graciously around town.

Christmas will be followed with a forward-looking attitude for the coming new year. Resolutions will be made in winter's presence to do better deeds with less faltering during the years ahead, to move, each in his own way, toward peace for all the world over.

Aren't we glad that winter came again to town this year? This wonderful, unchanging order in our changing, disordered world must indeed be a comforting balm to us all. Merry Christmas!

Christmas Is a Thousand Things

Lynda Bearden

Christmas is a thousand things . . .
A wondrous starlit night,
The songs of carolers in the street,
Or a child's eyes so bright.

Christmas is cold and warmth,
Forgiveness and tender smiles,
A handclasp firm, a letter flying
Across the snowy miles;

A trip back home, an open latch,
Gay ribbons, cards to send,
A candle in a window
That calls a stranger "friend";

The scent of pine on a Christmas tree,
Stockings hanging up,
The tinkle of a bell somewhere,
A coin dropped in a cup;

Christmas is a prayer,
As angel choirs sing again,
A plea renewed, an ancient hope
For "peace on earth, good will to men."

CHRISTMAS STOCKINGS HANG READY
ABOVE THE FAMILY FIREPLACE

Christmastime Snows

Irene Taylor

The snow falls like feathers,
So fluffy and white;
It lies on the ground
At a good sledding height.

Oh, bring out the boots,
Coats, gloves, and caps;
Button up buttons
And fasten down flaps.

Out with the sleds from their
Months stored away;
Off to the slopes
To frolic and play.

Snowballs are ready:
"That was a good throw!"
Snowmen and sledding—
Oh, wonderful snow!

Home late for supper,
Chilled from wet clothes;
How lovely are memories
Of Christmastime snows!

A BALSAM TREE WEARS A BLANKET OF SNOW,
BRISTOL, NEW HAMPSHIRE

FROZEN HILLTOP FOREST,
BLUE MOUNDS, WISCONSIN

Skating Pond

Edna Jaques

They dart about like water bugs
With waving arms and sprawling legs,
Some as graceful as the swans,
Others stiff as wooden pegs;
And yet the fun they have is worth
More than all the precious gold of earth.

The ice is clear as painted glass,
Bordered by heaps of drifted snow.
The winter sky above the trees
Almost as blue as indigo—
A setting lovely as a gem
Set in a vacant lot for them.

They swoop and dip and whirl and dart;
They fall with a thud and slide a bit.
They crawl on all fours like tiny bears,
Yet never seem to tire of it—
They're up and at it once again
Crusted with snow like frozen men.

Their little cheeks are warm and red,
Like apples on the rosy side.
Snowsuits of red and green and blue—
The little bodies tucked inside
Are warm as kittens wrapped in wool,
Lovely to look at, beautiful.

Here on this vacant lot is clearly heard
Young laughter merry as a lark,
The gay voice of a little girl,
A tiny dog's excited bark.
Here all the bells of heaven chime
Under the spell of wintertime.

The Joys of Wintertime

Mary A. Selden

Think about the wintertime,
What it means to you;
Turn your thoughts to childhood days,
Things you used to do.

Lean against the icy winds
In your heavy clothes;
Break off brittle icicles;
Strike a fencing pose.

Catch some snowflakes in your hand;
Taste their frosty lace;
Brush a pair of angel wings;
Tramp a circle chase.

Coasting down the nearest hill,
Steer your homemade sled;
Skate around a tiny pond
Flailing arms outspread.

Build a snowman; build a fort,
Snowballs stacked in mounds;
Clear a space to slide upon;
Play at "fox and hounds."

Run for home to help with chores;
Hear the old clock chime;
Live again and know again
The joys of wintertime.

CROSS COUNTRY SKIERS ENJOY THE WINTER LANDSCAPE,
COLORADO

Christmas of Long Ago

Earle J. Grant

Oh, for the kind of Christmas
That we had in days long ago.
With our old home in the country
Almost buried in sparkling snow.

Holly wreaths hung in the windows,
Each boasting a big bow of red;
Open fires blazed in every room
With stacks of logs in the woodshed.

The spruce tree stood in the parlor
Draped with cranberry ropes and popcorn;
Each branch was tipped with a candle
That dazzled our eyes Christmas morn.

Spicy scents drifted in from the kitchen,
Pearl-decked mistletoe crowned the door;
Loved ones gathered from far and near,
Gay greetings for each one in store.

Much can be said of modern Christmases,
But I treasure the ones long ago
At our old homestead in the countryside
Nestled deep in a white cloak of snow.

A COUNTRY DINING ROOM WITH CHRISTMAS TREE
STANDS READY FOR THE HOLIDAY FEAST

Festive December

Gladys Taber

APPLE TREE AND RED BARN CREATE A FESTIVE COUNTRY WINTER SCENE,
PLYMOUTH, NEW HAMPSHIRE

Winter comes to Stillmeadow, sifting down with the sifting snow. The snowfall gives a strange impermanence to the countryside, blurring the far hills, silvering the pond, tipping the mailbox with ermine. The air itself seems silver-white. When I go out to fill the bird feeders, starry flakes melt cool on my cheeks.

The chickadees chatter, nuthatches slide down tree trunks, blue jays cry angrily from the sugar maples. Juncos are almost under my feet. The relationship of birds and man is a rewarding one, for even the shiest birds respond to friendship. The bridge between me and mine is an easy one, composed of sunflower seeds, chick feed, raisins, bread crumbs, suet cakes. As I talk to the gathering wings, I am answered by the dipping towards my hands. I cannot help thinking that barriers between people—of all nationalities—should not be insurmountable, for human beings are of one species. Perhaps the secret is in personal giving. What is held out in the open hand means more than allotments.

As Christmas approaches, Erma helps me decorate Stillmeadow. Mistletoe, holly, and pine branches give a festive look to the old house. Gay greeting cards decorate two of the mantels, the corner cupboard where I keep the milk glass, and the bookshelves. Christmas candles go on the wide window ledges but never on the tree, for I am afraid they might start a fire. Bowls of fruit are temporary decorations, for the children start to eat the fruit as soon as they arrive for the holidays, and the bowl on the coffee bench has to be refilled several times a day.

The tree goes in the front living room, and we put our packages under it. Christmas Eve is my special time. When the children were growing up, Jill used to pop corn and set out the wooden dough trough, filled with nuts and polished apples, while I read Dickens' *A Christmas Carol* aloud. I know it by heart because it was read to me every Christmas when I was growing up. It was a link between the generations. Nowadays, however, the very young do not make for quiet reading. Even after they are tucked in they want a drink of water, or they lose their go-to-sleep rabbit over the crib wall, or *something*.

But after they finally go to sleep, the adults sit around the fire and talk. I have a chance to look at the three grown-up children—my daughter and Jill's son and daughter—and they are beautiful to me. Their young thoughtful faces have not really changed.

How far they have travelled since they were asking for a drink of water at bedtime! And how proud I am of them. Sometimes when I go out to the back kitchen to let Holly in, I imagine the drying bunny suits and mittens and hoods belong to my three. Time is a curious thing. Those bunny suits belong to Muffin, Anne, Jamie, and Betsy, and the larger snow outfits to the two older grandchildren (who also have ice skates, for fun on the pond).

This is an uneasy world, but in this holy time I find faith anew in the power of love and goodwill. My belief in goodness is not shaken. The babe born in the manger brought an enduring message to mankind. He was indeed to become the Prince of Peace, and is so still.

The snow stops falling, and the lovely light of a distant untroubled moon makes magic in swamp and meadow. The house settles into quiet. I go out with the cockers and Irish for a last look at night. On Christmas Eve my Honey—the golden cocker who companioned me for fourteen years—moves beside me. Jill stands in the lighted doorway. Remembrance is a form of meeting, says Gibran, and so it is.

Inevitably, as I turn out the lights and the embers die into ash, Connie comes softly down the stairs. "I just wanted to say what a lovely Christmas Eve, Mamma," she says. And this, of course, is my best present of all.

I think of neighbors I have never seen, all over the world, and pray for peace and goodwill for us all.

The Carolers

Ada B. Childs

The winter night was dark and cold until they sang,
Then with exultant melody the stillness rang.
We heard that song so old and dear,
"It Came upon a Midnight Clear,"
'Twas then we knew Christmas was near,
Sweet carolers!

A pause and then another burst of joyous song,
In which the tidings of His birth were borne along.
Just a small group, with lantern light,
They sang the sweet hymn "Silent Night,"
To make some lonely heart more bright,
Glad carolers!

Then flickering shadows crossed the snow—their slow retreat,
But bursts of praise came drifting back down the street.
Far off it comes, "Noel, Noel
Born is the King of Israel."
How sweet the tale in song you tell,
Young carolers!

CHRISTMAS LIGHTS BRIGHTEN A VICTORIAN HOME,
MIDDLETON, WISCONSIN

Nature Shares the Season

Fun in the Snow
LINDA NELSON STOCKS

A BEEF FARM APPEARS QUIET ON A WINTER DAY,
SOMERSET COUNTY, PENNSYLVANIA

In Lowly Places

Mrs. Roy L. Peifer

Sometimes
In lowly places
The most wondrous treasures
Are found,
The most brilliant
And precious diamonds
Buried in the blackest ground.

'Twas a strange place
To search for a King—
In a stable lowly and bare—
But shepherds from
Judean hills
Found the little
Lord Jesus there.

The Friendly Beasts

12th Century English carol

Jesus our brother, kind and good,
Was humbly born in a stable rude;
And the friendly beasts around him stood;
Jesus our brother, kind and good.

"I," said the donkey, shaggy and brown,
"I carried his mother uphill and down;
I carried her safely to Bethlehem town."
"I," said the donkey, shaggy and brown.

"I," said the cow, all white and red,
"I gave him my manger for his bed;
I gave him my hay to pillow his head."
"I," said the cow, all white and red.

"I," said the sheep, with curling horn,
"I gave him my wool for his blanket warm;
He wore my coat on Christmas morn."
"I," said the sheep, with curly horn.

"I," said the dove from the rafters high,
"Cooed him to sleep that he should not cry;
We cooed him to sleep, my mate and I."
"I," said the dove from the rafters high.

Thus every beast by some good spell,
In that dark stable was glad to tell
Of the gift he gave Emmanuel,
The gift he gave Emmanuel.

SUFFOLK EWES GRAZE THROUGH
SNOW OUTSIDE RUSTIC BARN

Country Barn Birdfeeder

Martha K. Bonner

This barn is for the birds! Securely fastened to a 20-inch square of plywood, this miniature barn is a traditional variation on today's popular birdhouses. It has a hinged roof that allows you to fill the inside with birdseed, and half-circles cut along the bottom sides of the barn provide automatic seed dispensing. The result is a charming feeding station that will fill your yard with beautiful birds all winter long.

Materials Needed:

Graphite paper
20-inch square of 1-inch plywood for base
3-foot piece of 1-x-12-inch pine shelving
5-foot piece of 1-x-6-inch pine shelving
Bandsaw or jigsaw
Sandpaper
$1\frac{1}{2}$-inch wood screws (#6)
Two $\frac{3}{4}$-inch wide brass hinges
Four 20-inch pieces of quarter round trim
$\frac{3}{4}$-inch wire brads (#18)
Forest green, gray, and brick red acrylic paints
Black medium-point paint pen
Brown shoe polish
Cloth rag
Craft glue
2 purchased miniature Christmas wreaths

Using graphite paper, transfer pattern for ends of barn to 1-x-12-inch piece of pine shelving and cut out with bandsaw or jigsaw. From remaining piece of 1-x-12-inch pine shelving, cut two 11-x-6-inch pieces for sides. From 1-x-6-inch piece of pine shelving, cut four $3\frac{3}{4}$-x-14-inch pieces for roof. Sand edges of all pieces smooth, including the plywood base.

For birdseed openings, measure and cut 3 half circles with a 1-inch radius on bottom of each side piece of barn, beginning $1\frac{3}{4}$ inches from side edges and spacing 1 inch between each half circle.

Attach sides of barn to inside edge of each end of the barn with wood screws, making sure sides and corners are even.

To make the barn roof, lay the two $3\frac{3}{4}$-x-14-inch pieces of pine shelving

together, with long edges of each piece parallel. Saw one side of each piece at a 70° angle. Referring to photograph, position the two roof pieces on top center of barn; then continue sanding sides until pieces fit together smoothly at their angled edges. Attach both top center roof pieces to ends of barn with wood screws.

For the sides of the barn roof, fit remaining roof pieces to sides of top center roof pieces in same manner as above. Attach one side piece of roof to ends of barn with wood screws. To complete roof, position one brass hinge 2 inches from each side of unattached roof piece and screw into place. Align angled edge of unattached roof piece with top center roof piece and screw hinges into place.

For edges of base, miter edges of quarter round trim pieces at a 45° angle. Position trim pieces along edges of base and nail in place using wire brads. Position barn in center of base and secure in place from underneath with wood screws.

Using acrylic paints, paint base and edges forest green, the barn brick red, and the roof gray. Let the paint dry thoroughly. Transfer the pattern for barn doors to one end of barn with the black paint pen; let dry. Lightly rub brown shoe polish over entire barn and base; then wipe excess polish with damp rag until the desired color is achieved.

To finish barn, glue purchased wreaths above doors.

COUNTRY BARN BIRDFEEDER WELCOMES HUNGRY WINTER BIRDS

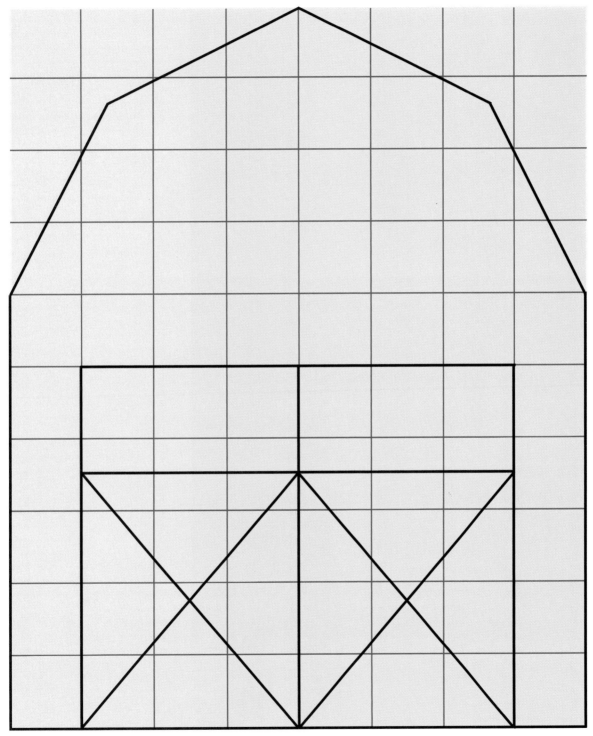

1 square equals 1 inch

The Legend of the Little Donkey

Grace E. Easley

There are many Christmas legends
And this is one of them,
About the little donkey
Mary rode to Bethlehem!

In his haste to start their journey,
Joseph bought what he could find,
And he led it from the market,
Never knowing it was blind!

As they had traveled all the morning,
And the sun had risen high,
Joseph said that they should rest
Beneath the trees nearby.

He dropped the rope the donkey wore,
And lifted Mary down,
But the little donkey stumbled
On a rock upon the ground.

And Joseph, looking closer,
Passed his hand before the eyes
Of the frightened little donkey;
But his heart could not despise

The animal's infirmity,
Remembering that he
At steady gait had borne the weight
Of Mary, patiently.

He gently took the donkey's rope
And led him 'neath the shade,
Where Mary sat upon a little
Blanket she had made.

36

HORSES MOVE THROUGH HEAVY SNOW AND FROST,
NEVADA

She softly whispered to him,
And he seemed to understand;
And he edged a little closer
As he nibbled at her hand.

And the small one never faltered
Through each long and weary mile,
And Joseph led him carefully,
For Mary was with Child!

And he held his head up proudly,
With frequent joyous sighs,
For his heart saw what he could not,
With his sightless little eyes.

And drawing near the city,
A weary Joseph found
No room except a stable
On the outskirts of the town.

So they shared it with the oxen,
And made a bed of hay,
So Mary and her newborn child
Could rest throughout the day.

And the little donkey stood against
The old rough stable wall,
Contented just to listen
To angel songs and all!

When suddenly about him
There appeared a wondrous light,
That fell across his rough brown coat
And blazed across the night.

And raising up His blessed hand,
The Child smiled tenderly,
And the little donkey staggered back—
Amazed, for he could see!

There are many Christmas legends,
And this is one of them;
They say it really happened,
Long ago in Bethlehem.

HORSES GRAZE BEFORE THE MAJESTIC BACKDROP OF
MT. SHASTA, CALIFORNIA

The Oxen

Thomas Hardy

Christmas Eve, and twelve of the clock.
"Now they are all on their knees,"
An elder said as we sat in a flock
By the embers in hearthside ease.

We pictured the meek, mild creatures where
They dwelt in their strawy pen;
Nor did it occur to one of us there
To doubt they were kneeling then.

So fair a fancy few would weave
In these years! Yet I feel,
If someone said on Christmas Eve,
"Come, see the oxen kneel,

"In the lonely barton by yonder coomb
Our childhood used to know,"
I should go with him in the gloom,
Hoping it might be so.

CATTLE IN SNOW,
MT. TOM, SIERRA NEVADA, CALIFORNIA

A MOURNING DOVE RESTS
IN LEAVES AND SNOW

The Birds

Czech Carol

From out of the wood did a cuckoo fly, *Cuckoo*;
He came to the manger with a joyful cry, *Cuckoo*;
He hopped, he curtsied, round he flew,
And loud his jubilation grew,
Cuckoo, Cuckoo, Cuckoo.

A pigeon flew over to Galilee, *Vrercroo*;
He strutted, and cooed, and was full of glee,
And showed with jeweled wings unfurled,
His joy that Christ was in the world,
Vrercroo, Vrercroo, Vrercroo.

A dove settled down upon Nazareth, *Tsucroo*,
And tenderly chanted with all his breath,
"O you," he cooed, "so good and true,
My beauty do I give to you—
Tsucroo, Tsucroo, Tsucroo."

A ROBIN PERCHES ON THE BRANCH
OF A HAWTHORNE TREE

Why the Robin's Breast
Is Red

Viola B. Gore

Did you ever hear the story
Why the robin's breast is red?
It happened, oh, so long ago
On Christmas Eve, 'tis said.

With his wing he fanned the tiny light
To keep the infant warm,
In that stable scene in Bethlehem
The night that Christ was born.

He got so close to that little flame
In his eagerness, 'tis said,
He scorched his breast, and ever since
The robin's breast is red.

A FEMALE CARDINAL BRIGHTENS THE WINTER WORLD

A Country Year

Lansing Christman

A countryman appreciates the way that winter settles down at last to a routine of steadiness. He likes the upland winter, the persistence of cold, the snows, and the driving winds. And outside a man's door, his hill-farm neighbors sweep in again from thicket and woodlot and slope to the dooryard birdfeeders and the windowsill.

These are tree sparrows and juncos, hairy and downy woodpeckers, nuthatches, and blue jays. There may be a wintering song sparrow and a meadowlark or two. Snow buntings move down now and then from the higher, windswept hills. Sometimes the purple finch and the goldfinch join in a breakfast on the farm lawn's spreading tables. While tree sparrows scratch in the seeds scattered on the crusts of snow, the nuthatches and woodpeckers hammer at the suet hung on the sheltered sides of pear trees and giant elms. But the most friendly visitor of all, a countryman thinks, is the black-capped chickadee which comes right up to the kitchen window and to a man's hands for crumbs of fried

cakes and broken nutmeats that have been provided on the clear, cold dawn of each new day.

These are a man's winter neighbors through the weeks of sun and snows, through the long, slow hours of driving winds and cold. They etch the stinging days with cheer and friendliness. Some of a countryman's most delightful hours have been spent with the birds. He hears a winter dawn filled with their constant notes and chirps. And it is hard for him to think of a season as too long or too sharp when he can start the day with the pleasing notes of a chickadee's call ringing out through the frost or a dense swirling snow.

Winter loses its heaviness. It becomes as beautiful and intricate as a star-shaped snowflake on a swollen lilac bud. Winter becomes as gentle as the wing of a tree sparrow in the dooryard hedge, as delicate as the touch of a chickadee's toes clinging to the fingers of a countryman's outstretched hand.

Winter's sharp ways are turned into a gentleness that befits the friendly little chickadee, ready to take flight after a breakfast of delicacies in the homemade birdhouse that swings softly in a wind that has worked its way around the corner of the veranda, a wind that never quite reaches to the shelter of the kitchen door. A man who feeds the birds can find the hills of snow as friendly as a summer meadowland of timothy and bloom. Winter's heaviness becomes as light as a wing and as lovely as a song.

CARDINALS PERCH ON THE
BRANCHES OF A CEDAR TREE

Winter Cheer

LaVerne P. Larson

Although the sky is dark and gray
And snow is on the ground,
It seems with every passing day
I hear a joyful sound.

It wakes me in the morning
When dawn is peeping through,
I hear it, oh, so often
To cheer me on anew.

'Tis my tiny chickadee friends
Who brave the cold and snow
To sing their happy melodies
And set my heart aglow.

The birds are very grateful
For the gifts of good I bring,
Yet it seems to be so little
For the lovely songs they sing.

MOUNTAIN CHICKADEE BIRDHOUSE,
COLORADO

AN EASTERN FOX SQUIRREL
CARRIES AWAY A STOLEN APPLE

Winter Animals

Henry David Thoreau

Usually the red squirrel waked me in the dawn, coursing over the roof and up and down the sides of the house, as if sent out of the woods for this purpose. In the course of the winter I threw out half a bushel of ears of sweet corn, which had not got ripe, onto the snow crust by my door, and was amused by watching the motions of the various animals which were baited by it. In the twilight and the night the rabbits came regularly and made a hearty meal. All day long the red squirrels came and went, and afforded me much entertainment by their maneuvers. One would approach at first warily through the shrub oaks, running over the snow crusts by fits and starts like a leaf blown by the wind, now a few paces this way, with wonderful speed and waste of energy, making unconceivable haste with his trotters, as if it were for a wager, and now as many paces that way, but never getting on more than half a rod at a time; and then suddenly pausing with a ludicrous expression and a gratuitous somersault, as if all the eyes of the universe were fixed on him—for all the motions of a squirrel, even in the most solitary recesses of the forest, imply spectators as much as those of a dancing girl—wasting more time in delay and circumspection than would have sufficed to walk the whole distance—I never saw one walk—and then suddenly, before you could say Jack Robinson, he would be in the top of a young pitch pine, winding up his clock and chiding all imaginary spectators, soliloquizing and talking to the uni-

verse at the same time—for no reason that I could ever detect, or he himself was aware of, I suspect. At length he would reach the corn, and selecting a suitable ear, brisk about in the same uncertain trigonometrical way to the topmost stick of my woodpile, before my window, where he looked me in the face, and there sit for hours, supplying himself with a new ear from time to time, nibbling at first voraciously and throwing the half-naked cobs about; till at length he grew more dainty still and played with his food, tasting only the inside of the kernel, and the ear, which was held balanced over the stick by one paw, slipped from his careless grasp and fell to the ground, when he would look over at it with a ludicrous expression of uncertainty, as if suspecting that it had life, with a mind not made up whether to get it again, or a new one, or be off; now thinking of corn, then listening to hear what was in the wind. So the impudent little fellow would waste many an ear in a forenoon; till at last, seizing some longer and plumper one, considerably bigger than himself, and skillfully balancing it, he would set out with it to the woods, like a tiger with a buffalo, by the same zigzag course and frequent pauses, scratching along with it as if it were too heavy for him and falling all the while, making its fall a diagonal between a perpendicular and a horizontal, being determined to put it through at any rate—a singularly frivolous and whimsical fellow—and so he would get off with it to where he lived, perhaps carry it to the top of a pine tree forty or fifty rods distant, and I would afterwards find the cobs strewn about the woods in various directions.

A GRAY SQUIRREL STANDS BY A HOLLY
TREE ON A COLD WINTER DAY

Woodland Solitude

Mildred L. Jarrell

The woodland path lies white and deep,
Mysterious and chill;
The hush of winter now prevails,
So tranquil and so still.

The evergreens are bending low
Upon an ermine throne,
And trailing lace is stitched in place
On tiny pointed cones.

The wildlings huddle through the night,
All curled in furry beds;
While snowflakes weave a counterpane
Of white far overhead.

The hush of winter reigns supreme
And sets a tranquil mood,
For earth at early dawn still dreams
In woodland solitude.

A RED FOX AGAINST A COLORFUL
CARPET OF LEAVES

A Miserable, Merry Christmas

Lincoln Steffans

What interested me in our new neighborhood was not the school, nor the room I was to have in the house all to myself, but the stable which was built in the back of the house. My father let me direct the making of a stall, a little smaller than the other stalls, for my pony, and I prayed and hoped and my sister Lou believed that that meant that I would get the pony, perhaps for Christmas. I pointed out to her that there were three other stalls and no horses at all. This I said in order that she should answer it. She could not. My father, sounded, said that some day we might have horses and a cow; meanwhile the stable added to the value of the house. "Some day" is a pain to a boy who lives in and knows "now." My good little sisters, to comfort me, remarked that Christmas was coming; but Christmas was always coming and grownups were always talking about it, asking you what you wanted and then giving you what they wanted you to have. Though everybody knew what I wanted, I told them all again. My mother knew that I told God, too, every night. I wanted a pony and to make sure that they understood, I declared I wanted nothing else.

"Nothing but a pony?" my father asked.

"Nothing," I said.

"Not even a pair of high boots?"

That was hard. I did want boots, but I stuck to the pony. "No, not even boots."

"Nor candy? There ought to be something else to fill your stocking with, and Santa Claus can't fit a pony into a stocking."

That was true, and he couldn't lead a pony down the chimney either. But no. "All I want is a pony," I said. "If I can't have a pony, give me nothing, nothing."

Now I had been looking myself for the pony I wanted, going to stable sales, inquiring of horsemen, and I had seen several that would do. My father let me "try" them. I tried so many ponies that I was learning fast to sit a horse. I chose several, but my father always found fault with them. I was in despair. When Christmas was at hand I had given up all hope of a pony, and on Christmas Eve I hung up my stocking along with my sisters, of whom, by the way, I now had three. I haven't mentioned them or their coming because, you understand, they were girls, and girls, young girls, counted for nothing in my manly life. They did not mind me either; they were so happy that Christmas Eve that I caught some of their merriment. I speculated on what I'd get; I hung up the biggest stocking I had, and we all went reluctantly to bed to wait until morning. Not to sleep; not

right away. We were told that we must not only sleep promptly, we must not wake up until seven-thirty the next morning—or if we did we must not go to the fireplace for our Christmas. Impossible.

We did sleep that night, but we woke up at 6:00 A.M. We lay in our beds and debated through the open doors whether to obey till, say, half past six. Then we bolted. I don't know who started it, but there was such a rush. We all disobeyed; we raced to disobey and get first to the fireplace in the front room downstairs. And there they were, the gifts, all sorts of wonderful things, mixed up piles of presents; only, as I disentangled the mess, I saw that my stocking was empty; it hung limp; not a thing in it; and under and around it—nothing. My sisters had knelt down each by her pile of gifts; they were squealing with delight, till they looked up and saw me standing there in my nightgown with nothing. They left their piles to come to me and look with me at my empty place. Nothing. They felt my stocking; nothing.

I don't remember whether I cried at that moment, but my sisters did. They ran with me back to my bed and there we all cried till I became indignant. That helped some. I got up, dressed, and driving my sisters away, I went alone out into the yard, down to the stable, and there, all by myself, I wept. My mother came out to me by and by; she found me in my pony stall, sobbing on the floor, and she tried to comfort me. But I heard my father outside, he had come part way with her, and she was having some sort of angry quarrel with him. She tried to

comfort me; she besought me to come to breakfast. I could not; I wanted no comfort and no breakfast. She left me and went on into the house with sharp words for my father. . . .

After—I don't know how long—surely an hour or two—I was brought to the climax of my agony by the sight of a man riding a pony down the street, a pony and a brand-new saddle; the most beautiful saddle I ever saw, and it was a boy's saddle; the man's feet were not in the stirrups; his legs were too long. The outfit was perfect; it was the realization of all my dreams, the answer to all my prayers. A fine new bridle, with a light curb bit. And the pony! As he drew near, I saw that the pony was really a small horse, what we called an Indian pony. A bay, with black mane and tail, and one white foot, and a star on his forehead. For such a horse as that I would have given, I could have forgiven, anything.

But the man, a disheveled fellow with a blackened eye and a fresh-cut face, came along, reading the numbers on the houses, and, as my hopes—my impossible hopes—rose, he looked at our door and passed by, he and the pony, and the saddle, and the bridle. Too much. I fell upon the steps, and having wept before, I now broke into such a flood of tears that I was a floating wreck when I heard a voice.

"Say, kid," it said, "do you know a boy named Lennie Steffens?"

I looked up. It was the man on the pony, back again, at our horse block.

"Yes," I sputtered through my tears. "That's me."

"Well," he said, "then this is your horse. I've been looking all over for you and your house. Why don't you put the number where it can be seen?"

"Get down," I said, running out to him.

He went on saying something about "ought to have got here at 7:00; he told me to bring the nag here and tie him to your post and leave him for you . . ."

"Get down." I said.

He got down, and he boosted me up to the saddle. He offered to fit the stirrups to me, but I didn't want him to. I wanted to ride.

"What's the matter with you?" he said angrily. "What are you crying for? Don't you like the horse? He's a dandy, this horse. I know him of old. He's fine at cattle; he'll drive 'em along."

I hardly heard, I could scarcely wait, but he persisted. He adjusted the stirrups, and then, finally, off I rode, slowly, at a walk, so happy, so thrilled, that I did not know what I was doing. I did not look back at the house or the man; I rode off up the street, taking note of everything—of the reins, of the pony's long mane, of the carved leather saddle. I had never seen anything so beautiful. And mine! . . .

But that Christmas, which my father had planned so carefully, was it the best or the worst I ever knew? He often asked me that; I never could answer as a boy. I think now that it was both. It covered the whole distance from broken-hearted misery to bursting happiness—too fast. A grown-up could hardly have stood it.

THOROUGHBREDS GRAZE ON A WINTER DAY,
KENTUCKY

A SIBERIAN HUSKY ENJOYS DECEMBER'S SNOW

A Christmas Pup

Alice Leedy Mason

Oh, what an absolute delight!
Just see what happened Christmas night.
A tiny pup—cute, wiggly, smart—
Came right into my eager heart.

I said "hello" and picked him up;
He was such a naughty pup.
He yawned and tried to get away
Because he thought he'd rather play.

So much to see, so many lights,
A dozen other tempting sights;
He had to wrestle with the rug
Before he paused to give a hug.

He gave each ornament a sniff,
Then tore the bows from every gift.
Worn out at last, he came my way
And love came in my heart to stay.

A TINY GRAY AND WHITE KITTEN PLAYS NEAR
CHRISTMAS HOLLY

A Christmas Kitten

Alice Leedy Mason

Our Christmas kitten's really bright;
She's standing guard this Christmas night.
Sometimes she jumps from stair to stair,
Or hides beneath the rocking chair.

She's keeping watch from dusk till dawn;
Something moves and the chase is on!
Papers rustle in a box;
A search is made of Christmas socks.

A toy mouse, a catnip ball,
Some scraps of yarn out in the hall,
The Christmas creche, a cookie plate,
All these she must investigate.

But not just now; it's time for bed;
A place to lay her weary head.
Content this is the place for her,
She drops her guard and starts to purr.

A Festive
Countryside

Christmas Saltbox
LINDA NELSON STOCKS

Snow on a Hill

Mamie Ozburn Odum

Come, walk with me
To the tall, broad hill,
Which is now knee-deep in snow,
And see the white immaculate spread
That lies silently far below.

The bright sun casts
A shimmering gleam
On the blanket so soft and white;
It decks the earth with a magic cloak
Which silently fell in the night.

The great trees stand
Tall and bare,
As if the land were deep in sleep,
Outlining beauty far and near
For the world of man to reap.

The snow-white blanket
Lay regally
Around each plant, white and serene;
The hills and rocks were hidden
As if tucked beneath a dainty screen.

Standing upon the hill
In awe and wonder,
I drink of the beauty given free:
A miracle sent down from heaven
To nature lovers such as we.

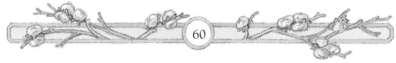

A VILLAGE RESTS UNDER A COVER OF SNOW,
PEACHAM, VERMONT

Winter Magic

Garnett Ann Schultz

I saw the winter magic
One cold December day,
In every little snowflake
So frolicky and gay;
I felt the winter coldness,
The wind so sharp and shrill,
And watched the snow fall heavily
To cover glen and hill.

I thrilled to winter's sparkle:
The world so big and white,
The stars like gorgeous diamonds
Upon the winter's night,
The evergreens so lovely,
Amid the ice and snow,
And little dots of silver
To add a special glow.

I laughed at winter's boldness,
The freezing morning air,
And marveled at the snowdrifts
She built just everywhere;
A masterpiece, that's certain,
A happy, pleasant thought,
And nothing quite to equal
The magic winter brought.

WAYSIDE MILL NESTLED IN SNOW,
MASSACHUSETTS

COUNTRY DINING ROOM PREPARED
FOR A CHRISTMAS FEAST

Christmas
Ferns

Hal Borland

The Christmas ferns remain green in the woods, bright patches of foliage which tempt the gatherer of holiday greens and remind me that anemones whitened a certain place last April and that violets purpled a particular spot.

There are a number of evergreen ferns, but this one, usually called *Aspidium acrostichoides* by the botanists, belongs in the old legends about the Nativity. Among the other wonders of that night, all the plants mingled in the hay in the holy stable put forth their blossoms in celebration. All, that is, except the ferns. And, say the legends, because the ferns failed to blossom and add their fragrance to that holy scene, they were condemned never again to bear flowers.

Thus the legends. But there must be more to it than that. Still thinking in terms of legendry, I believe that there must have been a frond or two of fern in the stable that tried to bloom that night, a few fronds that managed to turn green in celebration. It was the best they could do, being ferns. And since the utmost one can achieve is all that is ever asked, shouldn't the lowly ferns have been rewarded, even meagerly?

No legend of the Nativity should dwell on punishment, not even the legend of the ferns. They tried. They did their best. And that is why, it seems to me, some of them, like the Christmas fern, have their green fronds to offer in celebration now.

Christmas Icicle Legend

Mary Ann Putman

One night the Christ Child wandered
Through forest dark and cold;
There was no hut to shelter Him,
No angel's hand to hold.

Trees were bare. Their leaves were gone.
His young eyes spied the Pine,
Whose limbs, low hanging, sheltered Him
From piercing winds' sharp whine.

Caring for the Christ Child,
The Pine wept tears of joy
Freezing to icicles as they fell
Sheltering Mary's Boy.

Morning dawned sunlight's gold
In brilliance dazzling to behold.
And every Christmas icicles shine
In memory of this holy time.

A TINY PINE TREE HIDDEN AMONG ICY WEEDS,
CUMBERLAND FALLS STATE PARK, KENTUCKY

The Pines

Lorice Fiani Mulhern

How stately are the pines, how green!
Though unadorned by blossom or lovely leaves,
Into the very air they breathe
A fresh and tingling purity.

How they fill the forests free!
Fringing lakes and mountain tiers
With firs of all variety,
Firs that shed their softest needles
For seekers of tranquility.

At Yuletide many pines are captured
And enshrined indoors with love and care;
Their branches are entwined with lights
And enhanced with loveliest ornaments.

In winter they bear the heavy snow
As a sparkling, most becoming coat;
And when in spring the snow they shed,
They reveal a lasting youthfulness
That gives the world its freshness.

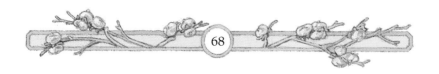

WINTER SUN SHINES THROUGH PONDEROSA PINES,
MOGOLLON RIM, ARIZONA

AMERICAN HOLLY ENCASED IN A
SPARKLING COVER OF ICE

The Story of
the Holly Sprig

Arthur Upson

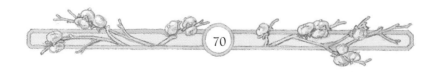

"I'd be the shiniest green,"
Wished once a sprig of holly,
"That e'er at Yule was seen,
And deck some banquet jolly!"

"I'd be the cheeriest red,"
Wished once the holly-berry,
"That e'er at board rich spread
Helped make the feasters merry!"

The life within them heard,
Down dark and silent courses,
For each wish is a word
To those fair-hidden sources.

All summer in the wood,
While they were riper growing,
The deep roots understood
And helped without their knowing.

In a little market stall
At Yule the sprig lay waiting,
For fine folk one and all
Passed by that open grating.

The Eve of Christmas Day
It had been passed by many,
When one turned not away
And bought it for a penny.

Hers was a home of care
Which not one wreath made jolly;
The only Christmas there
Was that sweet sprig of holly.

"Oh, this is better far
Than banquet!" thought the berry:
The leaves glowed like a star
And made that cottage merry.

Eucalyptus Wreath

Heidi T. King

Eucalyptus wreaths are a wonderful way to welcome the holidays, and because there are so many attractive varieties of natural and imitation materials available, crafting a holiday wreath allows you to add a personal touch to festive trimmings.

Materials Needed:
 Eucalyptus greens
 Grapevine wreath in desired size
 Flowers and berries for accents
 Ribbon in coordinating color
 Hot glue gun and glue sticks

To make a eucalyptus wreath, place the grapevine wreath on a flat surface and begin weaving eucalyptus between the vines. (A hot glue gun and glue sticks will secure the greenery to back of wreath.) Continue until the wreath base is covered with greenery, leaving traces of the grapevine visible.

 Position the flowers and berries where desired and weave between grapevines and the eucalyptus until secure. Embellish the wreath with a ribbon bow glued to the bottom.

A EUCALYPTUS WREATH WARMLY GREETS
HOLIDAY VISTORS

Snowflakes

Henry Wadsworth Longfellow

Out of the bosom of the air,
Out of the cloud-folds of her garments shaken,
Over the woodlands brown and bare,
Over the harvest fields forsaken,
Silent, and soft, and slow
Descends the snow.

Even as our cloudy fancies take
Sudden shape in some divine expression,
Even as the troubled heart doth make
In the white countenance confession,
The troubled sky reveals
The grief it feels.

This is the poem of the air,
Slowly in silent syllables recorded;
This is the secret of despair,
Long in its cloudy bosom hoarded,
Now whispered and revealed
To wood and field.

FOG ABOVE A SNOW-CARPETED ROAD,
NEVADA

A WARM KITCHEN FIREPLACE READY
TO WARD OFF WINTER CHILLS

December

Hal Borland

Last night we went out to walk on the frozen roads and when we came back I looked at the charts and found what I had suspected. Daylight is now at its minimum for the year. It will shorten only another two minutes or so between now and the Winter Solstice. The evening change, in fact, has already begun, for the year's earliest sunset is now past. Sunrise will continue to lag for another two weeks.

Thus the year balances its accounts, and what I said a few days ago about December's daylight stands only as a facetious comment. In our latitude we know that each year brings the time when not only the candle but the hearth fire must burn at both ends of the day, symbol not of waste but warmth and comfort. It is for this time, if we live close to the land, that we lay up the firewood and the fodder. Now we pay for the long days of Summer, pay in the simple currency of daylight. Hour for hour, the accounts are now balanced.

And yet, the short days provide their own bonus. The snows come, and dusk and dawn are like no other time of the year. We come to a long Winter night, as last night was, when the moon rides high over a white world and the darkness thins away. The full-moon night is as long as the longest span of sunlit day in midsummer. And the snowy world gleams with an almost incandescent shimmer.

Year to year, we remember the short days and tend to forget the long nights when the moon stands high over a cold and brittle white world. Not only the moon nights, but the star nights. Who would not cut wood and burn a candle for a few such nights each year?

Winter Night

Author Unknown

Outside, the icy wind with eerie sound
Sweeps through the trees and chants a minor strain,
Like one who on some endless quest is bound,
Seeking for that which he may never gain.

Grateful am I that I am housed tonight
Within four walls, the hearth fire flickering low;
You near to share with me in this delight
That soothes our senses with its genial glow.

We speak not any word to break the spell—
We fear to mar this perfect, golden hour;
Who called the winter drear? Do we not dwell
With beauty as lovely as a summer flower?

CHRISTMAS LIGHTS SHINE FROM AN ANTIQUE FARMHOUSE,
NEAR MARXVILLE, WISCONSIN

A HUSHED SILENCE COVERS THE LAND

Winter's Delight
LINDA NELSON STOCKS

Christmas in the Country

Inez Franck

The snowflakes ice the barnyard fences;
Inside, the embered hearth is warm;
The holly gathered from the woodlands
Is berry-red throughout the home.
The kitchen smells of ham and sausage,
And bread that's baked with loving care;
The cedar bowed with satin ribbons
Holds popcorn balls and angel hair.

The stars look down with quiet splendor
On candles gleaming through the pines;
The moon seems near in heaven's luster,
And how sublime its fullness shines!
Tonight the rural people mingle,
Unite their joys in glad refrain,
As carols ring beyond the chapel
With wondrous hope and peace again!

A COVERED BRIDGE SPANS THE FROZEN LAMOILLE RIVER AFTER A WINTER SNOWFALL,
WATERVILLE, VERMONT

Country Church at Christmastime

Ruth B. Field

Its cheery lights shine out across the snow
To make bright paths through the early dark,
And all the neighbors smile beneath the glow
Of tinseled tree topped with the silver spark
Of shining star: here peace and love abide.

And children's voices, rising sweet and clear,
Tell the story of glad Christmastide.
In the country church from far and near
Friends have gathered 'fore the Christmas tree
To hear the children sing and then recite
Their little poems; then eagerly they'll see
Old Santa Claus with cheeks so ruddy bright.

It seems the spirit of real Christmastime
In the country church fills each happy hour;
The angels sing above the old bell's chime,
And the star is bright above the small church tower.

GOLDEN LIGHTS SHINE IN ALTAR OF ST. JOHN'S CHURCH,
SALEM, NEW JERSEY

My First Christmas Tree

Hamlin Garland

When I was ten years old we moved to Mitchell County, in Iowa prairie land, and there we prospered in such wise that our stockings always held toys of some sort, and even my mother's stocking sagged with an occasional simple piece of jewelry or a new comb or brush. But the thought of the family tree remained the luxury of millionaire city dwellers; indeed, it was not until my fifteenth or sixteenth year that our Sunday school rose to the extravagance of a tree, and it is of this wondrous festival that I write.

The land about us was only partially cultivated at this time, and our district schoolhouse, a bare little box, was set bleakly on the prairie; the Burr Oak schoolhouse was not only larger, but it stood beneath great oaks as well and possessed the charm of a forest background through which a stream ran silently. It was our chief social center. There of a Sunday a regular preacher held "Divine Service" with Sunday school as a sequence. At night—usually on Friday nights—the young people met in "lyceums" as we called them, to debate great questions or to "speak pieces" and read essays; and here it was that I saw my first Christmas tree.

I walked to that tree across four miles of moonlit snow. Snow? No, it was a floor of diamonds, a magical world, so beautiful that my heart still aches with the wonder of it and with the regret that it has all gone—gone with the keen eyes and the bounding pulses of the boy.

Our home at this time was a small frame house on the prairie almost directly west of the Burr Oak grove, and as it was too cold to take the horses out, my brother and I, with our tall boots, our visored caps, and our long woolen mufflers, started forth afoot, defiant of the cold. We left the gate at a trot, bound for a sight of the glittering unknown. The snow was deep and we moved side by side in the grooves made by the hoofs of the horses, set-

AFTERNOON SUN SHINES ON A SMALL WHITE COUNTRY CHURCH,
NEAR WISCONSIN DELLS, WISCONSIN

ting our feet in the shine left by the broad shoes of the wood sleighs whose going had smoothed the way for us.

Our breath rose like smoke in the still air. It must have been ten below zero, but that did not trouble us in those days, and at last we came in sight of the lights, in sound of the singing, the laughter, the bells of the feast.

It was a poor little building without tower or bells and its low walls had but three windows on a side; and yet it seemed very imposing to me that night as I crossed the threshold and faced the strange people who packed it to the door. I say "strange people," for though I had seen most of them many times, they all seemed somehow alien to me that night. I was an irregular attendant at Sunday school and did not expect a present; therefore I stood against the wall and gazed with open-eyed marvelling at the shining pine which stood where the pulpit was wont to be. I was made to feel the more embarrassed by reason of the remark of a boy who accused me of having forgotten to comb my hair.

This was not true, but the cap I wore always matted my hair down over my brow, and then, when I lifted it off, invariably disarranged it completely. Nevertheless, I felt guilty—and hot. I don't suppose that my hair was artistically barbered that night—I rather guess that Mother had used the shears—and I can believe that I looked the half-wild colt that I was; but there was no call for that youth to direct attention to my unavoidable shagginess.

I don't think the tree had many candles, and I don't remember that it glittered with golden apples. But it was loaded with presents, and the girls coming and going in bright garments made me forget my own looks—I think they made me forget to remove my overcoat, which was a sodden thing of poor cut and worse quality. I think I must have stood agape for nearly two hours listening to the songs, noting every motion of Adoniram Burtch and Asa Walker as they directed the ceremonies and prepared the way for the great event—that is to say, for the coming of Santa Claus himself.

A furious jingling of bells, a loud voice outside, the lifting of a window, the nearer clash of bells, and the dear old Saint appeared (in the person of Stephen Bartle) clothed in a red robe, a belt of sleigh bells, and a long white beard. The children cried out, "Oh!" The girls laughed and clapped their hands. Then "Santa" made a little speech about being glad to see us all, but as he had many other places to visit, and as there were a great many presents to distribute, he guessed he'd have to ask some of the many pretty girls to help him.

They came up blushing, and a little bewildered by the blaze of publicity thus blown upon them. But their native dignity asserted itself, and the distribution of the presents began. I have a notion that the fruit upon the trees was mostly bags of popcorn and "corny copias" of candy, but as my brother and I stood there that night and saw everybody, even the rowdiest boys, getting something we felt aggrieved and rebellious. We forgot that we had come from afar—we only knew that we were being left out.

But suddenly, in the midst of our gloom, my brother's name was called, and a lovely girl with a gentle smile handed him a bag of popcorn. My heart glowed with gratitude. Somebody had thought of us; and when she came to me, saying sweetly, "Here's something for you," I had not words to thank her. This happened nearly forty years ago, but her smile, her outstretched hand, her sympathetic eyes, are all vividly before me as I write.

At last I had to take my final glimpse of that wondrous tree, and I well remember the walk home. My brother and I traveled in wordless companionship. The moon was sinking toward the west, and the snow crust gleamed with a million fairy lamps. The sentinel watchdogs barked from lonely farmhouses, and the wolves answered from the ridges. Now and then sleighs passed us with lovers sitting two and two, and the bells on their horses had the remote music of romance to us whose boots drummed like clogs of wood upon the icy road.

CHRISTMAS TREE, BIBLE, AND CANDLES

Country Choir Practice

Arthur Thatcher

It is on the eve of Christmas,
In the now-forgotten days;
Country church lamps have been lighted,
And its yard is full of sleighs.

Horses tied there to the hitchracks
Now are wearing strands of bells,
Tinkling with their restless movements
To enhance the sound that swells
From the organ in the chapel
And the carols of the choir.

They practice for tomorrow,
Seated near the blazing fire
Which is roaring now and snapping
In the tall, old Bridge Beach stove,
Stoked with wood chunks brought in autumn
From the nearby woodland grove.

And the picture in the darkness
That the lighted church now makes
Is the kind that leaves impressions
Which no memory forsakes.
It will come in recollection,
Through the years in many ways,
How the country church stood lighted
And its yard was full of sleighs.

SNOW BLOWS AND DRIFTS OUTSIDE ST. PHILLIPS EPISCOPAL CHURCH,
WISCASSET, MAINE

A CHRISTMAS MEAL AWAITS THE FAMILY

Christmas Candle Legend

Agnes B. Nickl

During the Christmas holidays the many decorations which adorn the windows and doors of homes are truly things of beauty. Each decoration has a meaning all its own. The legend of the Christmas candle, seen in so many of our windows at this beautiful season of the year, tells an inspiring story.

Many years ago, in a tidy little cottage on the edge of a village in Austria, a cobbler and his wife made their home. Their possessions were far from plentiful; but in spite of that, they shared what they had with others. Symbolic of their love and generosity for their fellow man was the lighted candle that they placed in the window of their humble cottage.

Over a number of years, war, with its companions famine and destruction, fell upon the land. This little village suffered; yet, through it all, the cobbler and his wife suffered less than the others.

The villagers were puzzled about this and talked among themselves. "Surely, there is something special about them," they said. "They are always spared from our misfortune. Let us put a candle in our window and see if that is the mysterious charm."

It so happened that the first night a candle was lighted in the window of every home was Christmas Eve. Before the first rays of the morning sun showed over the horizon, a messenger rode into the village to bring the great news: peace had come to the land.

That Christmas Day there was amazement and awe in the hearts of the humble villagers. And, as they thanked God for the blessings of peace, they said to one another, "Let us always remember to light candles on the evening of Christ's birth."

Many years have passed since this beautiful custom of placing a lighted candle in the window on Christmas Eve occurred. The custom has spread all over the world, sending forth a message of love, hope, and cheer.

CHRISTMAS LIGHTS WELCOME GUESTS TO VICTORIAN HOME,
BRISTOL, NEW HAMPSHIRE

Not Forgotten

Helen Welshimer

I shall place white candles
On every windowsill,
One to face the roadway,
And one to light the hill;

For I have read a story
Which says there was no light
In any house in Bethlehem
That other Christmas night.

Oh, should He come a wanderer,
This night, the Christ must see
That when I hung the stockings
And trimmed the Christmas tree,

I turned a shining moment,
From revelry and din,
To place a gracious welcome,
In case He passed my inn.

CANDLELIGHT BRIGHTENS THE BRANCHES OF A
WHITE PINE CHRISTMAS TREE

Candlelight

Brian F. King

Reluctant is the darkest night
To threaten bliss of candlelight;
For where the waxen tapers glow
Grim, questing shadows dare not go.

Soft candlelight betokens cheer
That beckons when the dusk appears
And sends its gentle, golden beams
To set bright silverware agleam.

It bathes within its subtle fire
The household things of heart's desire.
Where scented candles bring delight,
Children welcome stars of night.

And love is ever present where
The charm of candlelight is there;
For living reaches heights sublime
When candles glow at twilight time.

Christmas Eve

Reverend John W. Fehringer

The countryside in silence lay,
The trees all dressed in white;
The holly in the window gay,
Proclaimed this wondrous night.

The snowflakes softly came to earth
And stars shone bright above;
Hall and house were filled with mirth
And churches talked of love.

The icicles like crystal hung
And cold did bite the air;
Carols o'er the world were sung
And men did pray with care.

The window panes were white with frost,
The air was quiet and still;
The countryside in snow was lost,
From valley unto hill.

The still was broken by the sound
Of church bells ringing clear;
To tell to all that were around
That Christmas draweth near.

A STREET LAMP AND WREATH ANNOUNCE THE CHRISTMAS SEASON,
GATLINBURG, TENNESSEE

A Prayer at Christmas

Author Unknown

Give us the faith of innocent children,
That we may look forward
With hope in our hearts
To the dawn of happy tomorrows.

Reawaken the thought
That our most cherished desires will be realized—
The things closest to our hearts—
That we may come to an appreciation of the limitless joys
And bountiful rewards of Patience, Charity, and Sacrifice.

Above all, endow us with the spirit of courage,
That we may face the perplexities of a troubled world
Without flinching, imbued with the child-like faith
Which envisions the beautiful and inspiring things of life,
And restore the happy hours and experiences
So many of us foolishly believe are lost forever.

Give us faith in ourselves and faith in our fellow man,
Then the treasures and beauties of life that make man happy
Will spring from an inexhaustible source.

And at Christmas, when the hearts of the world
Swell in joyous celebration,
Let us cast aside the pretense of sturdy men
And live, if only for a day,
In the hope and joy we knew as children.

HAND-CARVED FIGURES DEPICT
THE SIMPLE BEAUTY OF THE NATIVITY

BACK HOME TO THE COUNTRY HEARTH

Blue Ice Pond
LINDA NELSON STOCKS

THE FRAZER HOUSE, BUILT IN THE 1880s,
SAN JUAN ISLANDS, WASHINGTON

Homeward Bound

Virginia Blanck Moore

My heart is homeward bound these days
Because it's Christmastime.
When I see windows gaily decked
And hear the carols chime;
When I meet parcel-laden folks
Returning smiles with smiles,
My heart goes winging straight across
The intervening miles
To home, to family, and to friends
That childhood days made dear,
To hometown streets where passersby
Greet one with welcoming cheer.
Though years go by, and decades, too,
Still I have always found
When Christmastime makes its approach
My heart is homeward bound.

FRESH WINTER SNOWFALL WHITENS THE HILLSIDES,
NEAR ARENA, WISCONSIN

The Road to Christmas

Garnett Ann Schultz

On the pleasant road to Christmas
Round a bend that leads to home,
There is laughter in the snowflakes
Such as none you've ever known.

You can see a lighted window
Ever bright and ever fair,
And the sounds of Christmas music
Fill the crisp, cold winter air.

Happy faces there to greet you
When at last the day is done,
With a welcome on the doorstep
Reaching out to everyone.

Lots of mistletoe and holly,
Little ones who still believe,
'Cause they know that dear old Santa
Will be there on Christmas Eve.

You will find the road to Christmas
Where your hopes and dreams come true,
And your heart will know the magic
That the season brings to you.

All the world's a little brighter
At this special time of year,
Peace on earth, because it's Christmas,
Bits of gladness, smiles of cheer.

May you know a joy this Christmas
That will fill your heart with love,
May your music be the music
Of the angels up above.

With the home fires softly glowing
May you find my wish sincere,
As the pleasant road to Christmas
Leads you through a bright new year.

Festive Pumpkin Pie

The holidays would not be complete without the luscious aroma of a pumpkin pie wafting from the country kitchen. In the following recipe, the old-fashioned pumpkin pie assumes a new look that everybody will love.

Combine ¾ cup sugar with 1 teaspoon cinnamon, ½ teaspoon cloves, ½ teaspoon ginger, ½ teaspoon nutmeg, and ½ teaspoon salt. Set aside. Beat 1 8-ounce package softened cream cheese until fluffy. Gradually stir in sugar/spice mixture. Add 3 eggs, one at a time, beating well after each addition. Fold in 2 cups canned or cooked pumpkin and 1 teaspoon vanilla. Pour into a 9-inch pie shell. Bake in a preheated 350° oven for 40 minutes or until knife inserted in center comes out clean. After 30 minutes of baking, place pecan halves around the edge of the pie for decoration. Chill before serving. Serves 8 to 10.

Cranberry Bread Pudding

Every well-dressed holiday table requires the traditional cranberry dish. This cranberry recipe, however, provides a different way of using the bright red berry: in a sweet and tempting dessert.

Combine 1¼ cups milk with ½ teaspoon salt, and ½ teaspoon vanilla. Stir in ¼ cup honey and 2 beaten eggs. Pour over 2 cups stale bread, cut in 1-inch cubes; mix well. Stir in 1 cup fresh cranberries. Pour into a shallow, greased 1½-quart baking dish. Bake in a preheated 350° oven 25 minutes or until firm. Serve warm with whipped cream. Serves 6.

FESTIVE RED WALLS SURROUND BEAUTIFULLY
DECORATED CHRISTMAS TREE

THE DECORATED DOORWAY OF A BED AND BREAKFAST
CHEERFULLY WELCOMES CHRISTMAS GUESTS

It Is Christmas Once More

Loretta Bauer Buckley

It is Christmas once more. Do you remember when your world was very young, how you jumped into bed and counted on your fingers just how many days it would be until that glorious day arrived? Lying snug and warm in your feather bed you saw a thousand glittering angel-topped trees in the dark; heard the prancing of Dasher and Dancer on the attic roof. Even the branches of the old maple, storm-tossed against your window, played a Yuletide melody.

There was so much to be done in the last few hours before Santa's visit that you scarcely took time to breathe. In the flurry of excitement Mother developed the art of moving in all directions at once and you had to be constantly shooed from underfoot.

The fragrance that came from the kitchen skyrocketed your anticipation of good things to come—mace, cinnamon, nutmeg, not to mention ginger cookies and fresh bread cooling on the table. The pantry bulged with vegetables, apples, and jars of golden fruit brought up from the cellar. Do you remember making sure there were spiced peaches because you liked those the best?

Bringing in wood for the fireplace in the "company" parlor became a pleasure. And shovelling a path through the snow from the porch to the woodshed was a cherished chore. The spirit of giving and doing filled every inch of your small frame.

And what fun it was going into the woods to chop down the Christmas tree! Though the icy wind stiffened your nose and ears, the glow in your heart more than made up for the pain you knew. As the tree was placed in the barn, you were certain you heard a baby's cry come from the hayloft. You had prepared a crib—and did not miracles happen at Christmastide? Frankincense and myrrh were strange-sounding gifts, so you left part of a nameless joy you felt there beside the small manger.

In the parlor, the redolence of the tall fir, as the warmth of the room touched it, cast a perfume you said you would never forget. And you promised to remember always the ruby red cranberry chains that swung gaily from its emerald branches.

The ritual of hanging your stocking shattered your heart into diamond-like fragments of happiness. You could never find a word for that enchanted moment—even to this day. Then to bed, and though the floor was as cold as the pond on which you hoped to try your new skates, you did not leave out a single prayer. The first one was for the Baby Jesus, and the last for the safety of St. Nicholas.

The eve of Christmas is upon us once again. Candles of memory flame brightly over the years and the miles of drifted snow. In your dreams tonight you may hear the cry of the newborn King as you heard it in childhood's golden hours: songs of the herald angels, shepherds' sandaled steps on Bethlehem's starlit road. And you may wake to a world grown miraculously new, beautiful beyond belief, because a little Child came into it with the gift of perfect love for all men.

FESTIVE NAPKINS AND PLACEMATS IN COUNTRY BASKET

A Basket Full of Placemats

Heidi T. King

In the festive colors of Christmas, with the look and feel of an old-fashioned country home, this basket full of placemats makes a wonderful gift for a friend and is also a useful item to make and to have on hand for casual Christmastime entertaining.

Materials Needed:

    1½ yards 45-inch quilted cotton in Christmas color or print

    2 yards 45-inch plain or printed cotton in coordinating color

    Two 6-yard packages of extra-wide double-fold bias tape

    Thread to match fabric colors

    Farmer's basket with wooden handle

(*Note*: Allow ½ inch for seam allowance.)

Draw a pattern by following the dimensions of first diagram and cut out. (Note: opening for basket handle is a curve cut in 2" at top and 3" down.) Lay pattern on folded quilted fabric and cut through both thicknesses. When fabric is opened out, it should look like diagram 2.

    With right sides together, bring B corners up to A corners. Stitch along edge. Press open seams. Stitch along bottom opening (side C in diagram 3). Repeat for other side. Following instructions on package, attach bias tape to basket liner around the opening for basket handles. Then attach bias tape around edge of basket liner, allowing 6 inch ties on each side of handle openings. Place liner inside basket and tie ends around handles. Cut placemats in 14 x 20-inch ovals (as shown in diagram 4). For each placemat, cut 1 piece from both quilted and plain material and place wrong sides together. Sew bias tape around edges. Cut four 18-inch squares for napkins from printed cotton fabric. Finish with a ¼-inch rolled hem.

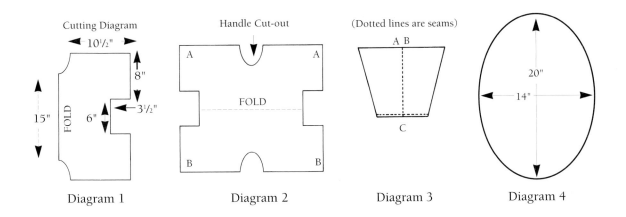

Cutting Diagram — 10½" — 8" — 15" — FOLD — 6" — 3½"

Diagram 1

Handle Cut-out — A — A — FOLD — B — B

Diagram 2

(Dotted lines are seams) — A B — C

Diagram 3

20" — 14"

Diagram 4

Christmas Is

Diana Smith Watts

Christmas smells like bayberry candles, pine trees,
Logs burning in the fireplace—
Like popped corn, and plum pudding with flaming sauce,
Like turkey and cranberries.

Christmas feels like holly wreaths pricking your fingers,
Fragile, egg-like tree ornaments
And silky spun-glass angel hair,
Like sticky seals and smooth-silk ribbon.

Christmas sounds like church bells chiming,
Children laughing, voices singing "Silent Night"—
Like hustling feet and small bells tinkling,
Like snow crunching underfoot.

Christmas tastes like crisp apples and sweet tangerines,
Pumpkin pie and fruit cake,
Eggnog and cracked nuts,
Like date cookies and hot chocolate.

Christmas looks like holly stretched across the streets,
Like mistletoe in the doorways and bright packages on the floor,
Like stars and creches and animals in humbled awe by their manger,
Wherein lies a different, smaller Being.

Christmas is the knowledge in our hearts
That, through the Word made Flesh in the manger of Bethlehem,
We know we belong to God and cannot perish;
That we have a perfect, permanent refuge and home.

DECORATED COUNTRY LIVING ROOM
WITH BRICK FIREPLACE

Grandmother's House

Adam N. Reiter

Away with a dash and jingling bells,
In a two-horse cutter sleigh;
The children are off to Grandmother's house,
For an old-style Christmas Day.
There's sparkling beauty o'er valley and hill,
And a nip in the frosty air;
There's hearty cheer in the neighbor's hail,
And gladness everywhere.

A grand old place is Grandmother's house,
Massive and rambling and low,
Nestled and hid in the lee of a hill,
And wrapped in a blanket of snow.
Down the lane and over the bridge,
Then on to the opened door;
Greeted by Rover's welcoming bark,
And those who've arrived before.

Grandmother's kitchen is all aglow
With a friendly cheer of its own,
With singing kettle and glowing hearth,
That beams with the warmth of home.
Grandfather sits in his easy chair
With his favorite pipe alight;
The clan has gathered—the children are home:
It's Christmas and "all is right!"

HORSE-DRAWN SLEIGH GLIDES ACROSS THE WINTER LANDSCAPE,
TELLURIDE, COLORADO

Cross-Stitch Quilt
Jar Toppers

Martha K. Bonner

A mix of quilting and cross-stitching is cleverly utilized in the patterns for these charming jar toppers, which turn jars of homemade jams and jellies into wonderful, personalized Christmas gifts for friends and family.

Materials Needed (to make one jar topper):

    One 4-inch square of 14-count white aida cloth
    Embroidery floss (see color charts on following pages)
    Canning jar with flat lid and jar ring
    One 4-inch square of thin quilt batting
    Craft glue
    Hot-glue gun and glue sticks
    ½ yard ⅜-inch wide ribbon to match floss

Center design on aida cloth and work according to chart, using two strands of floss. Using flat jar lid as a guide, center and trace circle around finished cross-stitch design and cut out. Repeat for quilt batting.

    With craft glue, lightly glue batting to top of flat jar lid; then center cross-stitch design over quilt batting. Place jar ring over flat lid design.

    Hot-glue ribbon around outer edge of ring, trimming ends diagonally to prevent ravelling. Tie remaining ribbon into a bow and hot-glue to jar ring over ends of ribbon.

FESTIVE CROSS-STITCHED LIDS TOP JARS
READY FOR CHRISTMAS GIVING

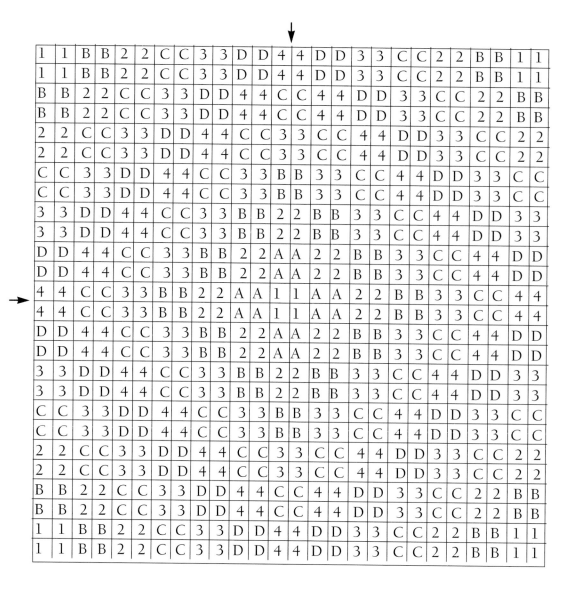

```
1 1 B B 2 2 C C 3 3 D D 4 4 D D 3 3 C C 2 2 B B 1 1
1 1 B B 2 2 C C 3 3 D D 4 4 D D 3 3 C C 2 2 B B 1 1
B B 2 2 C C 3 3 D D 4 4 C C 4 4 D D 3 3 C C 2 2 B B
B B 2 2 C C 3 3 D D 4 4 C C 4 4 D D 3 3 C C 2 2 B B
2 2 C C 3 3 D D 4 4 C C 3 3 C C 4 4 D D 3 3 C C 2 2
2 2 C C 3 3 D D 4 4 C C 3 3 C C 4 4 D D 3 3 C C 2 2
C C 3 3 D D 4 4 C C 3 3 B B 3 3 C C 4 4 D D 3 3 C C
C C 3 3 D D 4 4 C C 3 3 B B 3 3 C C 4 4 D D 3 3 C C
3 3 D D 4 4 C C 3 3 B B 2 2 B B 3 3 C C 4 4 D D 3 3
3 3 D D 4 4 C C 3 3 B B 2 2 B B 3 3 C C 4 4 D D 3 3
D D 4 4 C C 3 3 B B 2 2 A A 2 2 B B 3 3 C C 4 4 D D
D D 4 4 C C 3 3 B B 2 2 A A 2 2 B B 3 3 C C 4 4 D D
4 4 C C 3 3 B B 2 2 A A 1 1 A A 2 2 B B 3 3 C C 4 4
4 4 C C 3 3 B B 2 2 A A 1 1 A A 2 2 B B 3 3 C C 4 4
D D 4 4 C C 3 3 B B 2 2 A A 2 2 B B 3 3 C C 4 4 D D
D D 4 4 C C 3 3 B B 2 2 A A 2 2 B B 3 3 C C 4 4 D D
3 3 D D 4 4 C C 3 3 B B 2 2 B B 3 3 C C 4 4 D D 3 3
3 3 D D 4 4 C C 3 3 B B 2 2 B B 3 3 C C 4 4 D D 3 3
C C 3 3 D D 4 4 C C 3 3 B B 3 3 C C 4 4 D D 3 3 C C
C C 3 3 D D 4 4 C C 3 3 B B 3 3 C C 4 4 D D 3 3 C C
2 2 C C 3 3 D D 4 4 C C 3 3 C C 4 4 D D 3 3 C C 2 2
2 2 C C 3 3 D D 4 4 C C 3 3 C C 4 4 D D 3 3 C C 2 2
B B 2 2 C C 3 3 D D 4 4 C C 4 4 D D 3 3 C C 2 2 B B
B B 2 2 C C 3 3 D D 4 4 C C 4 4 D D 3 3 C C 2 2 B B
1 1 B B 2 2 C C 3 3 D D 4 4 D D 3 3 C C 2 2 B B 1 1
1 1 B B 2 2 C C 3 3 D D 4 4 D D 3 3 C C 2 2 B B 1 1
```

Color Key

(All numbers are for DMC floss)

	Lid 1		Lid 2
1	326	1	351
2	309	2	352
3	335	3	353
4	3326	4	754
A	336	A	500
B	312	B	561
C	334	C	562
D	775	D	564

@	@	@	#	#	#	$	$	$	%	%	%	¢	¢	¢	¢	¢	¢	¢	¢	¢	¢	¢	¢
@	@	@	#	#	#	$	$	$	%	%	%	¢	¢	¢	¢	¢	¢	¢	¢	¢	¢	¢	¢
@	@	@	#	#	#	$	$	$	%	%	%	¢	¢	¢	¢	¢	¢	¢	¢	¢	¢	¢	¢
@	@	@	#	#	#	$	$	$	%	%	%	&	&	&	&	&	&	&	&	&	&	&	&
@	@	@	#	#	#	$	$	$	%	%	%	&	&	&	&	&	&	&	&	&	&	&	&
@	@	@	#	#	#	$	$	$	%	%	%	&	&	&	&	&	&	&	&	&	&	&	&
@	@	@	#	#	#	$	$	$	%	%	%	*	*	*	*	*	*	*	*	*	*	*	*
@	@	@	#	#	#	$	$	$	%	%	%	*	*	*	*	*	*	*	*	*	*	*	*
@	@	@	#	#	#	$	$	$	%	%	%	*	*	*	*	*	*	*	*	*	*	*	*
@	@	@	#	#	#	$	$	$	%	%	%	X	X	X	X	X	X	X	X	X	X	X	X
@	@	@	#	#	#	$	$	$	%	%	%	X	X	X	X	X	X	X	X	X	X	X	X
@	@	@	#	#	#	$	$	$	%	%	%	X	X	X	X	X	X	X	X	X	X	X	X
X	X	X	X	X	X	X	X	X	X	X	X	%	%	%	$	$	$	#	#	#	@	@	@
X	X	X	X	X	X	X	X	X	X	X	X	%	%	%	$	$	$	#	#	#	@	@	@
X	X	X	X	X	X	X	X	X	X	X	X	%	%	%	$	$	$	#	#	#	@	@	@
*	*	*	*	*	*	*	*	*	*	*	*	%	%	%	$	$	$	#	#	#	@	@	@
*	*	*	*	*	*	*	*	*	*	*	*	%	%	%	$	$	$	#	#	#	@	@	@
*	*	*	*	*	*	*	*	*	*	*	*	%	%	%	$	$	$	#	#	#	@	@	@
&	&	&	&	&	&	&	&	&	&	&	&	%	%	%	$	$	$	#	#	#	@	@	@
&	&	&	&	&	&	&	&	&	&	&	&	%	%	%	$	$	$	#	#	#	@	@	@
&	&	&	&	&	&	&	&	&	&	&	&	%	%	%	$	$	$	#	#	#	@	@	@
¢	¢	¢	¢	¢	¢	¢	¢	¢	¢	¢	¢	%	%	%	$	$	$	#	#	#	@	@	@
¢	¢	¢	¢	¢	¢	¢	¢	¢	¢	¢	¢	%	%	%	$	$	$	#	#	#	@	@	@
¢	¢	¢	¢	¢	¢	¢	¢	¢	¢	¢	¢	%	%	%	$	$	$	#	#	#	@	@	@

Color Key

(Unless otherwise specified, all numbers are for DMC floss.)

	Lid 3			Lid 4
@	701		@	3326
¢	701		#	335
#	666		$	309
&	666		&	326
$	701 and 002C		¢	775
*	701 and 002C		%	334
%	666 and 002C		*	312
X	666 and 002C		X	336

(For $, *, %, and X use two strands
of Kreinik # 002C in addition to two
strands of DMC floss.)

Note: All DMC stitches should be worked with double strands.

121

CHARMING ANTIQUE TOYS REST BENEATH
CHRISTMAS TREE IN A COUNTRY INN

An Old-Fashioned Christmas

Patricia Mongeau Hofmiller

I'd like to push the calendar
Back fifty years or so
And celebrate my Christmas
As they did so long ago.

A tree of green would grace my room
With candles shining bright,
And popcorn strings and homemade things
Would fill me with delight.

I'd make a gift or two for each
One in my family
And hide them until Christmas,
When I'd place them 'neath the tree.

The snow that fell upon the ground
Would last all winter long;
I'd ride a one-horse open sleigh
And sing a Christmas song.

The family would go to church
Through snow on Christmas morn
And listen to the story of
When Jesus Christ was born.

They wouldn't have the worries of
A shopping tour each day
To outdo one another
With their gifts on Christmas Day.

Christmas many years ago
Was a splendid thing:
A simple day to celebrate
The birth of Christ our King!

A ROARING FIRE WARMS A CHRISTMAS EVE

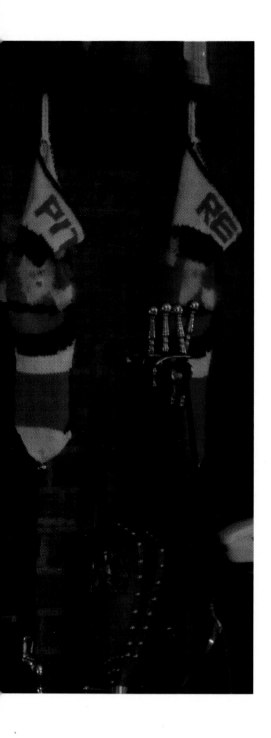

Jeweled
for
Christmas

Leila Pier King

You have known, O beautiful tree,
Skies of velvet in the crimson dawn,
Intimate winds and sounds that betray
The motherless and bewildered fawn.

You have known communion with rain
And sun, and the solitude of storm;
Through years of growing, standing serene,
You nested the birds and kept them warm.

Transfigured now, O beautiful tree,
Jeweled for Christmas, the time of His birth,
Chosen with love for your grace as true
As silver tones of a child's sweet mirth.

You live in this room, your beauty unhurt,
Your heaven-most branch illumed by the light
Of a deathless star, which hallows the heart,
This lovely night, this holy night.

A BURLAP STOCKING CAPTURES THE FEELING
OF CHRISTMAS IN THE COUNTRY

Country Christmas Stocking

Nancy J. Worrell

Filling stockings with goodies and surprises is a delightful family tradition to keep at Christmastime, and it becomes even more special when the stockings are lovingly hand-crafted, yet it will take only minutes to complete.

Materials needed:

½ yard of 45-inch-wide burlap

Khaki sewing thread

#18 tapestry needle

1 skein 4-ply red acrylic yarn

Using the diagram below and extending legs to a total of 15 inches, cut two stocking pieces out of the burlap. If desired, decorate one side of stocking with scraps of bandana fabric, buttons, and decorative trim. With raw edges aligned and wrong sides together, zigzag-stitch stocking together along outside edges, leaving top open.

Thread the tapestry needle with two 36-inch strands of red yarn. Buttonhole stitch around the outside edges of the stocking, beginning and ending two inches from top. (Buttonhole stitches should conceal the zigzag stitching.)

Fold the top down 2 inches, forming a cuff, and buttonhole stitch around top of stocking along fold.

For hanging loop, braid three 16-inch pieces of yarn together to form an 8-inch braid. Thread the tapestry needle with braided yarn and stitch through top of stocking at rear fold. Knot ends to form a loop for hanging.

Unravel stocking cuff 1½ inches around edge to make fringe.

1 square equals 1 inch

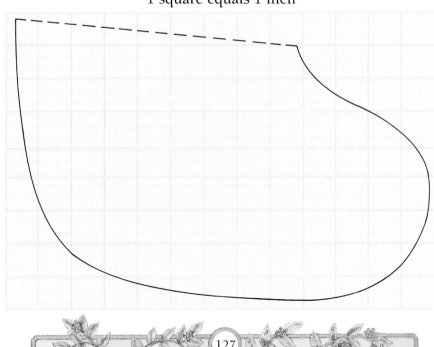

The More the Years

Douglas Malloch

The more the years the more we all remember
Our yesterdays, the things that used to be;
The summertime seems fairer in December,
And roses fade, but not from memory.
Youth has so much, and thinks how empty age is,
With only dreams of things so long ago;
But we who sit and turn life's lovely pages—
What joy we know!

The more the years the more our sorrows soften;
The more the years, the more they turn to gold.
Yes, life's a tale, though told however often,
That fairer grows with every time it's told.
Youth has today, and youth is young and clever,
Age only yesterdays of smiles and tears;
And yet the past grows lovelier forever,
The more the years.

STACKED FIREWOOD READY FOR
WOODSTOVE AND FIREPLACE

The Heart Goes Home

Grace V. Watkins

Always the heart goes home on Christmas Eve,
Goes silently across a continent,
Or mountains, or the seas. A heart will leave
The glitter of a city street and, sent
By something deep and timeless, find the way
To a little cottage on a country hill.

And even if the little cottage may
Have disappeared, a heart will find it still.

The smile of tenderness upon the faces,
The simple words, the arms secure and strong,
The sweetness of the well-remembered places—

All these a heart will find and will belong
Once more to country hills, however far,
And sense the holy presence of the Star.

A FARM RESTS BENEATH A BLANKET OF DECEMBER SNOW,
NEAR BLACK EARTH, WISCONSIN

131

The House That Is Your Heart

James Dillet Freeman

Take this Christmas Day to go
A little way apart,
And with your hands prepare
The house that is your heart.

Brush out the dusty fears, brush out
The cobwebs of your care,
Till in the house that is your heart,
It's Christmas everywhere.

Light up every window with love,
And let your love shine through,
That they who walk outside may share
The blessed light with you.

Then will the rooms with joy be bright,
With peace the hearth be blessed,
And Christ himself will enter in
To be your Christmas guest.

FESTIVE CHRISTMAS LIGHTS ADORN CAPE NEDDICK LIGHT,
YORK, MAINE

It Began in a Manger

Candles in the Window
LINDA NELSON STOCKS

Simplicity

Hal Borland

Not the least of the wonders we celebrate today is the simplicity surrounding the Birth itself. A carpenter named Joseph went with his young wife up from Nazareth to Bethlehem, the town of his fathers, to enroll for taxation as the governing Romans had ordered. Joseph and Mary arrived late and weary to find that the inn was crowded; so they took shelter in the stable with the other latecomers. Second best, but humble travelers could not choose. It was shelter. And there in the stable the Child was born.

Thus the simple beginnings. Add the shepherds on the night hills, the appearance of the angel, their journey to the stable, and it still remains one of the least adorned of all the great stories we cherish. It is as simple as was the Man himself and His teachings. As simple as the Sermon on the Mount, which still stands, in its essentials, as the summary of the belief of free men of good will everywhere.

There were the night hills with the little town among them. And in a stable there was born One who came to speak to multitudes about freedom and justice and fundamental right. One who spoke in a simple tongue, in terms of the beasts of the land, the birds of the air, the lilies of the fields, and man's responsibility to man. The kings and captains were marching up and down the land, in full panoply, even as He was being born. But it is His simple words that endure, not theirs; and it is the Birth at the stable that we solemnly commemorate, not the gathering at the crowded inn.

MT. MANSFIELD RISES BEHIND COUNTRY VILLAGE,
WATERBURY CENTER, VERMONT

FROZEN SOUTH FORK OF SOUTH PLATTE RIVER,
COLORADO

The Shepherd's Tale

Josephine Powell Beaty

You ask me child, to tell once more
The story of the star,
While watching with my father's flocks
I saw shine from afar.

It was my task to tend the sheep
To guard them night and day.
The nearest town was Bethlehem,
And that was miles away.
I never left this pasture land,

These fields are all I know—
The little streams, the rolling hills,
The nooks where flowers grow.
I saw the star rise in the East
And brighter grow each night,
I turned my eyes away in fear
Before its searching light.
A wind came rushing through the night;
And when I looked again,
Strange shapes were moving in the sky—
I saw a host of men.

And everywhere I looked there were—
North, west, and south and east—
A vast and mighty throng of men,
The greatest and the least.
For some had crowns and some had chains,
A plow, a sword, a ring,
And all of them were kneeling down
As though before a king.

The shades of night can never give
The bright hues of the sun;
Though every face was different,
The starlight made them one.
Since then, new springs have come and gone
And many a winter's snow,
And yet I never shall forget
That night of long ago.
They tell me there were other lads
Who must have seen the gleam;
Later, when they told of it,
They thought it was a dream.

A dream, they said; it might have been,
And yet this much I know,
The world has waited for a light
To guide men here below.
And I maintain forever more
It was a wondrous sight—
That mighty host of men who knelt
Together on that night.

Come to the Manger

Emma S. McLaughlin

A gray dove perched in the rafters,
A new star blazed in the sky,
From the shadows surrounding the manger
Echoed an infant's cry.
Great love was shared in the stable,
Infinite peace filled the night,
A luminous flame touched faith's candle
And mankind walked in the light.

A STAR SHINES ABOVE A TINY, SNOW-COVERED CABIN,
SAN JUAN MOUNTAINS, COLORADO

A SPARKLING LAYER OF ICE COVERS THE LANDSCAPE,
NEAR BARNEVELD, WISCONSIN

Manger Scene

Elisabeth Johnson

I think I shall speak softly lest
This beauty be defiled,
Lest stillness be disturbed and I
Should wake
A sleeping Child.

He is to waken all too soon—
So let Him rest tonight,
Protected by our love and this
Unwavering vigil light.

Within the shadows of the room
The oxen eyes are deep
With pity for
So small a King,
So gravely lost in sleep.

Three kings have travelled far tonight,
Their royal gifts to lay
In reverence at His baby feet,
Half hidden in the hay.

They kneel in worship at His side,
For they are old and wise . . .
But she who gazes on His face
Has only mother eyes.

Let us speak quietly for fear
The holy watch they keep
Be broken;
Let our words be hushed . . .
A Baby is asleep.

The Shepherds

And there were in the same country shepherds abiding in the field, keeping watch over their flock by night. And, lo, the angel of the Lord came upon them, and the glory of the Lord shone round about them: and they were sore afraid.

And the angel said unto them, Fear not: for, behold, I bring you good tidings of great joy, which shall be to all people.

For unto you is born this day in the city of David a Saviour, which is Christ the Lord. And this shall be a sign unto you; Ye shall find the babe wrapped in swaddling clothes, lying in a manger.

And suddenly there was with the angel a multitude of the heavenly host praising God, and saying,

Glory to God in the highest, and on earth peace, good will toward men.

Luke 2:8-14

ICE-COVERED TREES FILTER THE WINTER SUNRISE

Hymn for the Nativity

Edward Thring

Happy night and happy silence downward
Softly stealing, softly stealing over land and sea;
Stars from golden censers swing a silent eager
Feeling down on Judah, down on Galilee;
And all the wistful air and earth and sky
Listened, listened for the gladness of a cry.

Holy night, a sudden flash of light its way is
Winging; angels, angels, all above, around;
Hark, the angel voices, hark, the angel voices
Singing; and the sheep are lying on the ground.
Lo, all the wistful air and earth and sky,
Listen, listen to the gladness of the cry.

Wide, as if the light were music, flashes adoration
"Glory be to God, nor ever cease,"
All the silence thrills, and speeds the message of
Salvation: "Peace on earth, good will to men of peace."
Lo, all the wistful air, and earth and sky,
Listen, listen to the gladness of the cry.

Holy night, thy solemn silence evermore enfoldeth
Angels' songs and peace from God on high:
Holy night, thy watcher still with faithful eye
Beholdeth wings that wave, and angel glory nigh,
Lo, hushed is strife in air and earth and sky,
Still thy watchers hear the gladness of the cry.

Praise Him, ye who watch the night, the silent
Night of ages: praise Him, shepherds, praise the Holy
Child; praise Him, ye who hear the light, O Praise
Him, all ye sages; praise Him, children,
Praise Him meek and mild.
Lo, peace on earth, glory to God on high,
Listen, listen to the gladness of the cry.

A STAR ANNOUNCES CHRISTMAS OVER SNOW-COVERED LANDSCAPE,
COLORADO

A Christmas Carol

Josiah Gilbert Holland

There's a song in the air!
There's a star in the sky!
There's a mother's deep prayer
And a baby's low cry!
And the star rains its fire while the choirs sing,
For the manger of Bethlehem cradles a King.

There's a tumult of joy
O'er the wonderful birth,
For the Virgin's sweet Child
Is the Lord of the earth,
Ay! the star rains its fire and the choirs sing,
For the manger of Bethlehem cradles a King.

In the light of that star
Lie the ages impearled;
And that song from afar
Has swept over the world.
Every hearth is aflame and the choirs sing
In the homes of the nations that Jesus is King.

We rejoice in the light,
And we echo the song
That comes down through the night
From the heavenly throng.
Ay! we list to the lovely message they bring,
And we greet in His cradle our Saviour and King.

A WINTER SUNRISE OVER FROZEN LAKE,
LAKE TAHOE, NEVADA/CALIFORNIA

Lo! The Light!

Elizabeth Landeweer

Above the manger stood a star,
A star all wondrous white;
And all about His lowly bed
There welled a flood of light.

It bathed the stable in its glow,
It shone round Mary's head;
And on the kneeling shepherds' cloaks
Its radiant beams were shed.

Star of the world! Through time and space
It flames in glory bright
To make man's pathway through the years
A pilgrimage of light.

It shines for us—that light still shines!
No cloud can dim its spark;
Its radiance blossoms bright with joy,
A beacon in the dark.

The path leads on, the path leads up;
We walk it mile by mile,
And lo! The light His love has lit
Grows brighter all the while.

Oh, never doubt it shines for you,
Though skies seem dark and low—
Keep looking up, keep lifted up,
Somewhere a star will show!

Let not your heart be trouble-filled.
The darkest night must clear,
And life be glad and life be sweet,
For lo! The light is here!

Because of Christmas

Grace M. Walker

The precious Christmas story
Lives on through all the years,
And mother love is kinder,
Because of Mary's tears.

And earth is still a haven
For men who seek the right,
Life still has its depth of love
Because of Christmas night.

If men could meet at Christmas
Around the manger bed
And catch the Christmas spirit
The hungry would be fed,
And little children everywhere
Would know true love and tender care,
Because of Christmas.

CONGREGATIONAL CHURCH STANDS ON WHITENED WINTER STREET,
HEBRON, NEW HAMPSHIRE

THE LIGHTS OF CHRISTMAS WARM A ROOM

The Christmas Spirit

Virginia Blanck Moore

When the Christmas spirit springs to life
In the human heart each year,
The world becomes, for a little time,
A haven of love and cheer.

The poor of body are clothed and fed,
And the lonely know once more
The warmth of hearing a welcoming knock
On a too long silent door.

For these few days we remember well
That all of mankind is kin,
Bound by love of the babe who found
No room in that long-ago inn.

But the day goes by, and the spirit dies,
So busy with living are we,
And the poor and the lonely are left once more
In hunger and apathy.

I have been guilty, too, God knows,
Too busy to lend a hand,
Too busy to stop for a friendly chat,
Too busy to understand.

"No more, no more let this happen to me,
Dear Lord," I earnestly pray.
"Let me keep the Spirit the whole year through
As bright as it is today."

Keeping Christmas

Henry Van Dyke

It is a good thing to observe Christmas Day. The mere marking of times and seasons, when men agree to stop work and make merry together, is a wise and wholesome custom. It helps one to feel the supremacy of the common life over the individual life. It reminds a man to set his own little watch, now and then, by the great clock of humanity which runs on sun time.

But there is a better thing than the observance of Christmas Day, and that is keeping Christmas.

Are you willing to forget what you have done for other people, and to remember what other people have done for you; to ignore what the world owes you and to think what you owe the world; to put your rights in the background and your duties in the middle distance, and your chances to do a little more than your duty in the foreground; to see that your fellow men are just as real as you are, and try to look behind their faces to their hearts, hungry for joy; to own that probably the only good reason for your existence is not what you are going to get out of life, but what you are going to give to life; to close your book of complaints against the management of the universe, and look around you for a place where you can sow a few seeds of happiness—are you willing to do these things for even a day? Then you can keep Christmas.

Are you willing to stoop down and consider the needs and desires of little children; to remember the weakness and loneliness of people who are growing old; to stop asking how much your friends love you, and ask yourself whether you love them enough; to bear in mind the things that other people have to bear on their hearts; to try to understand what those who live in the same house with you really want, without waiting for them to tell you; to trim your lamp so that it will give more light and less smoke; and to carry it in front, so that your shadow will fall behind you; to make a grave for your ugly thoughts, and a garden for your kind feelings, with the gate open—are you willing to do these things even for a day? Then you can keep Christmas.

Are you willing to believe that love is the strongest thing in the world—stronger than hate, stronger than death—and that the blessed life which began in Bethlehem nineteen hundred years ago is the image and brightness of Eternal Love? Then you can keep Christmas.

And if you keep it for a day, why not always? But you can never keep it alone.

A CHRISTMAS WREATH AND RIBBON
WITHSTAND THE WINTER COLD

God Bless
Your Christmas

Hazel Adams

God bless your Christmas wherever you are
And keep your courage bright;
For the spirit of man is the candle of God,
And it burns in the darkest night.

God bless your Christmas wherever you are
And keep you strong in faith;
For the Spirit of God is the refuge of man
And the light is His dwelling place.

AUTHOR INDEX

Adams, Hazel B.
    "God Bless Your Christmas" 158
Bearden, Lynda
    "Christmas Is a Thousand Things" 12
Beaty, Josephine Powell
    "The Shepherd's Tale" 138
Bonner, Martha K.
    Country Barn Birdfeeder.........................32
    Cross-Stitch Jar Toppers.......................118
Borland, Hal
    Christmas Ferns..65
    December 77
    Simplicity..136
Buckley, Loretta Bauer
    "It Is Christmas Once More" 111
Childs, Ada B.
    "The Carolers" 24
Christman, Lansing
    A Country Year......................................45
Easley, Grace E.
    "The Legend of the Little Donkey" 36
Engle, Paul
    An Iowa Christmas...................................8
Fehringer, Reverend John W.
    "Christmas Eve".....................................98
Feltham, Harriet
    "It's Christmastime"..................................6
Field, Ruth B.
    "Country Church at Christmastime".......84
Finch, Rosalyn Hart
    Christmas Is the Best Day of Winter..........10
Franck, Inez
    "Christmas in the Country"....................82
Freeman, James Dillett
    "The House That Is Your Heart" 132
Garland, Hamlin
    My First Christmas Tree 86
Gore, Viola B.
    "Why the Robin's Breast Is Red".............43
Grant, Earle J.
    "Christmas of Long Ago".........................20
Hardy, Thomas
    "The Oxen"..40
Hofmiller, Patricia Mongeau
    "An Old-Fashioned Christmas".............123
Holland, Josiah Gilbert
    "A Christmas Carol" 149
Jaques, Edna
    "Skating Pond" 17
Jarrell, Mildred L.
    "Woodland Solitude" 50
Johnson, Elisabeth
    "Manger Scene" 143
King, Brian F.
    "Candlelight" 97
King, Heidi T.
    A Basket Full of Placemats....................113
    Eucalyptus Wreath 72
King, Leila Pier
    "Jeweled for Christmas" 125

Landeweer, Elizabeth
    "Lo! The Light".....................................151
Larson, LaVerne P.
    "Winter Cheer".......................................46
Longfellow, Henry Wadsworth
    "Snowflakes"...74
Malloch, Douglas
    "The More the Years" 128
Mason, Alice Leedy
    "A Christmas Kitten"..............................56
    "A Christmas Pup" 57
McLaughlin, Emma S.
    "Come to the Manger"..........................140
Moore, Virginia Blanck
    "Homeward Bound"...............................105
    "The Christmas Spirit" 155
Mulhern, Lorice Fiani
    "The Pines" 68
Nickl, Agnes B.
    Christmas Candle Legend.......................93
Odum, Mamie Ozburn
    "Snow on a Hill" 60
Peifer, Mrs. Roy L.
    "In Lowly Places" 29
Putman, Mary Ann
    "Christmas Icicle Legend" 66
Reiter, Adam N.
    "Grandmother's House".........................116
Schultz, Garnett Ann
    "Winter Magic".......................................62
    "The Road to Christmas".......................107
Selden, Mary A.
    "The Joys of Wintertime" 18
Steffans, Lincoln
    A Miserable, Merry Christmas 52
Taber, Gladys
    Festive December 22
Taylor, Irene
    "Christmastime Snows".........................14
Thatcher, Arthur
    "Country Choir Practice" 90
Thoreau, Henry David
    Winter Animals.......................................48
Thring, Edward
    "Hymn for the Nativity" 146
Upson, Arthur
    "The Story of the Holly Sprig"................70
Van Dyke, Henry
    Keeping Christmas.................................156
Walker, Grace M.
    "Because of Christmas".........................152
Watkins, Grace V.
    "The Heart Goes Home" 130
Watts, Diana Smith
    "Christmas Is".......................................114
Welsheimer, Helen
    "Not Forgotten" 95
Worrell, Nancy J.
    Country Christmas Stocking 127

TITLE INDEX

A Basket Full of Placemats 113
"Because of Christmas" 152
"The Birds" 42

"Candlelight" 97
"The Carolers" 24
Christmas Candle Legend............................93
"A Christmas Carol" 149
"Christmas Eve" 98
Christmas Ferns 65
"Christmas Icicle Legend" 66
"Christmas in the Country" 82
"Christmas Is" 114
"Christmas Is a Thousand Things" 12
Christmas Is the Best Day of Winter.................10
"A Christmas Kitten"...................................56
"Christmas of Long Ago" 20
"A Christmas Pup".......................................57
"The Christmas Spirit"................................155
"Christmastime Snows".................................14
"Come to the Manger"................................140
Country Barn Birdfeeder 32
"Country Choir Practice"..............................90
Country Christmas Stocking.......................127
"Country Church at Christmastime" 84
A Country Year 45
Cranberry Bread Pudding...........................108
Cross-Stitch Jar Toppers.............................118

December 77

Eucalyptus Wreath 72

Festive December 22
Festive Pumpkin Pie....................................108
"The Friendly Beasts" 30

"God Bless Your Christmas".........................158
"Grandmother's House" 116

"The Heart Goes Home" 130
"Homeward Bound" 105

"The House That Is Your Heart" 132
"Hymn for the Nativity" 146

"In Lowly Places" 29
An Iowa Christmas 8
"It Is Christmas Once More" 111
"It's Christmastime 6

"Jeweled for Christmas" 125
"The Joys of Wintertime" 18

"Keeping Christmas" 156

"The Legend of the Little Donkey" 36
"Lo! The Light" 151

"Manger Scene" 143
A Miserable, Merry Christmas 52
"The More the Years" 128
My First Christmas Tree................................86

"Not Forgotten"..95

"An Old-Fashioned Christmas".....................123
"The Oxen"..40

"The Pines"..68
"A Prayer at Christmas" 100

"The Road to Christmas" 107

"The Shepherd's Tale" 138
Simplicity 136
"Skating Pond" 17
"Snow on a Hill" 60
"Snowflakes" 74
"The Story of the Holly Sprig".......................70

"Why the Robin's Breast Is Red" 43
Winter Animals...48
"Winter Cheer"...46
"Winter Magic"...62
"Winter Night" 78
"Woodland Solitude".....................................50

ART & PHOTO CREDITS

4-5, Linda Nelson Stocks; 7, Ed Cooper Photo; 9, Dianne Dietrich Leis; 10, William Johnson/Johnson's Photography; 13, Jessie Walker Photography; 15, William Johnson/Johnson's Photography; 16, Ken Dequaine; 19, Grant Heilman/Grant Heilman Photography; 21, Jessie Walker Photography; 22, William Johnson/Johnson's Photography; 25, Ken Dequaine; 26-7, Linda Nelson Stocks; 28-9 Larry Lefever/Grant Heilman Photography; 31, Larry Lefever/Grant Heilman Photography; 34, Bob Schwalb; 37, Linda Dufurrena/Grant Heilman Photography; 39, Ed Cooper Photo; 41, Ed Cooper Photo; 42, Barry L. Runk/Grant Heilman Photography; 43, Gay Bumgarner; 44, Adam Jones; 45, Gay Bumgarner; 47, Grant Heilman/Grant Heilman Photography; 48, Gay Bumgarner; 49, Gay Bumgarner; 51, Gay Bumgarner; 55, Daniel E. Dempster; 56, Barry L. Runk/Grant Heilman Photography; 57, Gay Bumgarner; 58-9, Linda Nelson Stocks; 60-1, William Johnson/Johnson's Photography; 63, Dianne Dietrich Leis; 64, Jessie Walker Photography; 67, Adam Jones; 69, Dick Dietrich Photography; 70, Gay Bumgarner; 73, Bob Schwalb; 75, Linda Dufurrena/Grant Heilman Photography; 76, Superstock, Inc.; 79, Ken Dequaine; 80-1, Linda Nelson Stocks; 82-3, William Johnson/Johnson's Photography; 85, Jeffrey Sylvester/FPG, International; 87, Ken Dequaine; 89, Daniel E. Dempster; 91, William Johnson/Johnson's Photography; 92, Jessie Walker Photography; 94-5, William Johnson/Johnson's Photography; 96, Barry L. Runk/Grant Heilman Photography; 99, Daniel E. Dempster; 101, Gerald Koser; 102-3, Linda Nelson Stocks; 104, Ed Cooper Photo; 106, Ken Dequaine; 109, Jessie Walker Photography; 110, Kintner House Inn, Corydon, IN, Daniel E. Dempster; 112, Bob Schwalb; 115, Jessie Walker Photography; 117, Jessie Walker Photography; 119, Bob Schwalb; 122, Daniel E. Dempster; 124, Superstock, Inc.; 126, Bob Schwalb; 129, Runk/Schoenberger/Grant Heilman Photography; 131, Ken Dequaine; 133, William Johnson/Johnson's Photography; 134-5, Linda Nelson Stocks; 137, William Johnson/Johnson's Photography; 138, Grant Heilman/Grant Heilman Photography; 141, Ed Cooper Photo; 142, Ken Dequaine; 144-5, Linda Anderson; 146, Adam Jones; 147, Adam Jones; 148-9, Grant Heilman/Grant Heilman Photography; 150, Ed Cooper Photo; 153, William Johnson/Johnson's Photography; 154, Larry Lefever/Grant Heilman Photography; 157, Thomas Hovland/Grant Heilman Photography.

A	1
B	2
C	3
D	4
E	5
F	6
G	7
H	8
I	9
J	0